Clearing Away the Wreckage of the Past:

A Task Oriented Guide for Completing Steps 4 through 7

John Leadem, MSW
Elaine Leadem, MSW

Table of Contents

Welcome

Much of our early lives were shaped by disappointment and heartache. Childhood was marred by parental neglect and abuse. The traumatic exposure to violence, sexual abuse, and spiritual deprivation set the stage for a tumultuous adolescence and young adulthood that was void of hope. Each of us had entered the age of reason with little more than an oath to "never end up like" the role models of our childhood. It was not even a solemn oath. By the time we had reached adult life we discovered yet another lie of our childhood caregivers that had been used to silence our inquiries. Each of us had questioned, whenever possible, the reason for the crazy or erratic behavior we witnessed all around us. Neither of us were told why the people in our lives were so mean but we were promised that we would "know better" when we were older. By the time we entered adult life we had managed to become older but we did not know any better and we certainly were not any wiser.

We do not propose that our embattled childhood and harrowing adolescent years were any more challenging than scores of other children raised in homes and extended families that were riddled with addiction or other forms of dysfunction. In many ways we suspect that we were not any less prepared for the challenges of adult life and marriage than the average young couple. We, like many of the "forgotten" children of the era, came to the altar on our wedding day with a good deal of injury and brokenness. A formula for disaster, you might say. You would be right to assume that a union of our two souls would probably ignite a powder keg of character defects that would ultimately dissolve our flimsy resolve to be different than our caregivers. It would have been a safe bet to wager that the marriage would not last a year. Some wondered if it would make it through the honeymoon.

If you had bet against us you would have lost because we will soon celebrate 35 years of married life "IN" sobriety. You would have lost the bet, not because it was fool hardy for you to bet against a "match made in heaven" but because it was a union that began in sobriety. The 12 Steps and the recovery culture that offered some the promise of rehabilitation was more of a habilitation opportunity for us as it was our first opportunity to obtain any real health at all. We virtually grew up in the 12 Step rooms. The 12 Steps became the bond that held us together. Many marriages that endure great disappointment and hardship, and escape an early divorce, often do so because of the pathological bond that keeps them enmeshed through compatible defects of character.

We have shared many *compatible defects of character*[1] over the years that have required both personal and professional attention but the overwhelming reason we have remained together and are celebrating rather than just enduring life is because we believe in and practice the 12 Steps. The spiritual principles inherent in the 12 Steps represent the core of our respective value systems and serve as the basis for our plan for sober living. We have personally benefitted from and believe in therapy but the fundamental personality and spiritual changes we have been rewarded with have come from our commitment to the 12 Steps. Our commitment to and success with integrating these principles into our therapeutic work with clients, whenever possible, has lead us to develop guides that eliminate some of the confusion surrounding the mechanics of actually completing a particular Step.

Clearing Away the Wreckage of the Past: A Task Oriented Guide for Completing Steps 4 through 7 is offered as an adjunct to the inspiration you are receiving from your recovery support system and a practical format for working through the steps collaboratively with your therapist or spiritual advisor. Your purchase of this guide also serves as an invitation to contact us, if you need, for further explanation of any component or task that you find challenging. You can call us at Leadem Counseling & Consulting Services, PC (732-797-1444) or visit our website at www.leademcounseling.com where you can ask us a question about the guide or obtain additional information on a variety of recovery issues. You do not need to make the journey alone. We hope the guide will serve you as it has served us.

We are with you in spirit.

John and Elaine Leadem

Section 1: Preparing for the Housecleaning

Chapter 1: Housecleaning Tools

The classic recovery text *Alcoholics Anonymous*[2] introduces the idea of a "personal housecleaning" as the first leg in a "course of vigorous action" that the reader is enjoined to begin immediately following the surrender decision in the Third Step. The reader is further warned that without such a "... strenuous effort to face, and to be rid of, the things in ourselves which had been blocking us ..." that the freedom found in the Third Step " ... could have little permanent effect." The guide is designed to provide you with the tools for that personal housecleaning.

Clearing Away the Wreckage of the Past: A Task Oriented Guide For Completing Steps 4 through 7 was designed for a single person but groups of people can and have come together for the purpose of providing each other with mutual support and guidance in the completion of these vital steps. Partners in a committed relationship have used the material to enhance the quality of their recovery programs through a model that the authors have titled a *Shared Program of Recovery©*[3]. We have provided a brief overview of the guide through a description of each of the three sections. We begin with a brief overview of the three sections before introducing the housecleaning aids offered in the guide to help you work through Steps 4 through 6.

Section Overviews

The guide is divided into the following three sections:

Section 1: Preparing for the Housecleaning

The first section helps to insure that you will be undertaking the process of clearing away the wreckage of the past from the basis of a well-developed recovery foundation. This section introduces the task centered approach to completing Steps 4 and 6 that the authors have used with recovering addicts and their co-addicted family members for the past 38 years in a variety of professional settings. The introspective tools and step sponsor prompts that will help you remain emotionally and spiritually grounded while remaining on task are introduced conceptually. As additional preparation for the coming step work, Section 1 will provide an overview of the first three steps, explain what is meant by a housecleaning and conclude with important pre-requisites for you to consider prior to undertaking the task work.

Section 2: Putting an End to the Secrets – Steps 4 & 5

This next section introduces the components associated with the housecleaning tasks involved in the completion of a searching and fearless moral inventory. Sequential tasks are provided to guide you through each of the four components of the Fourth Step complete with examples and detailed analysis of the action oriented tasks involved. The section concludes with a brief introduction to the Fifth Step.

Section 3: Character Building – Steps 6 & 7

The third section provides measureable tasks to aid in the understanding and identification of your shortcomings and the development of healthy coping strategies to replace defects of character that you have developed to meet life's emotional challenges. Comprehensive examples are included to help you to get the maximum benefit from your efforts and to enhance your ability to communicate your needs to members of your support group and your therapist or spiritual advisor.

Task Centered Approach

There are many different approaches to the completion of the steps in the Twelve Step process of recovery from addiction and co-addiction. The task-centered approach presented in this guide has evolved through many modifications during the collective recovery and professional experience of the authors that spans over 75 years. The methodology found in the tasks has been derived from the authors' development and evaluation of the strategies that have anecdotally proven to be helpful for individuals that become emotionally blocked during introspective work. The step-by-step guidance that the task centered approach employs has made the completion of difficult steps like 4 and 6 manageable for individuals that struggle to put their thoughts on paper or have difficulty remembering their own story.

The Fourth and Sixth Steps are deeply probing inventories into your past and represent penetrating analyses of your personality. Your honest exploration will stir emotions and challenge your spirit. The following introspective tools will aid you along the way.

Introspective Tools

Throughout the guide you will be prompted to take proactive care of your emotional and spiritual needs through the use of the Introspective Tools. They may not show up every time you need them so use them as a model for maintaining self-care throughout your work. They are introduced below in more detail for your reference.

Introspective Prayer

In introspective prayer we have learned to move beyond the prayers of our childhood and to present ourselves before the God of our understanding or higher power, if you prefer. We learned to talk with our God as we would a dear and loving friend rather than to recite prayers we had committed to rote memory. Those repetitive prayers can provide helpful balance and focus throughout the day, but we needed to get comfortable with presenting ourselves to God in a way that would make it easier for us to hear, in meditation, the response. We do not try to hide those parts we find objectionable; for we have found that our higher power loves us because of our warts and problems and not in spite of them. We discovered that the humility we were seeking was there in abundance when we made a decision to open ourselves completely to our higher power and began to reveal ourselves to others.

You will be encouraged to return to prayer throughout the inventory guide. We suggest that you get comfortable with a one-on-one sharing with your God. It does not create an obstacle if your concept of a God is a Power greater than yourself. Regardless of your definition of God or a higher power, it may prove very helpful to spend time working on improving your spiritual communication. Do not be afraid. We are not going to recommend a particular method of prayer that requires specialized training. You will not have to undertake any physical contortions to place yourself in a "prayerful" posture and you will not need candles or mood music. Your spiritual communication will improve with practice and the peace you gain through sober life experiences.

The simplest way to improve your level of spiritual communication is through the use of letter writing. The model we suggest is writing a "Dear higher power" letter. In your correspondence spill out your heart through the honest description of what is on your mind and how you are feeling. It becomes prayer when you read it aloud to yourself or another person.

When the guide suggests you take some time to pray, do so quietly in your thoughts, aloud in a conversation with your higher power, or purposefully in your "Dear higher power" letters. You might want to hold onto those letters to read to the person you share your Fifth Step with or for future reference. The guide will offer examples of prayer. They are not intended to be a prescription, only a model. Your own wording will be much more valuable. If you have not developed or do not prefer a prayer life, respond to the prompt by having a mental or written conversation with a member of your support group whose recovery you respect or with a trusted friend.

Meditative Reflection

In meditation we look to improve our ability to identify and understand the direction that our higher power is trying to communicate to us. It has been said that prayer is speaking and meditation is listening to God. As you mature in your recovery, we are sure that you will find that the time spent practicing meditation will become invaluable. This guide will ask you to meditate on feelings you have developed through your work on each of the components. Your life experiences are recorded in your memory in a variety of ways that include colors, smells, sounds, and feelings – so use them all.

There are many methods available in psychological and spiritual literature to aid you in your use of meditation in your daily recovery. This guide will not introduce or review the various meditation methods. In meditation, as with prayer, there is no right or wrong way to meditate. The object of meditation is to develop a better understanding of God's will for us and to enjoy the peace that our increased knowledge brings.

The guide will introduce two forms of meditation. One style of meditation will encourage you to use your feeling memories to identify past life experiences in which wrongs have occurred. You are directed in the Tasks to imagine that you are in the experience you are describing in your entries. Doing so will help to activate your feeling memory. The recollection of these life experiences is important because they rekindle long-standing resentments without us being aware of the connections. We say to ourselves "here we go again" and we prepare to feel the same as we did in the past because our feeling memories have been triggered. Past life experiences will often contain the emotionally traumatic events that represent the birthplace of many of our most resilient defects of character.

When asked to recall feeling memories you will need only to allow yourself to remember the experience you have been writing about and the feelings you have will awaken past experiences in which similar feelings were felt. The Feeling Words (Appendix F) at the end of the guide will prove helpful in the process of naming the feelings; however, the name we assign to a feeling is not as important as the honest expression of the breadth and depth of our emotional reactions.

The second form of meditation will use guided imagery to help evaluate and focus your efforts. The scenes created are intended to promote inner calm and to strengthen your commitment to the Tasks ahead. The meditations in each case will follow a sample prayer. An alternative to either prayer or meditation is a have a period of quiet reflection on the sources of your gratitude or the exposure to soothing music or art.

Written Accountability

The guide encourages you to record your work on paper because writing promotes the highest level of accountability. We have found most people have a tendency to alter the material that they have amassed in their inventories when they are doing their Fifth Step, unless they have written it. All too often we have found ourselves diluting the intensity of an experience when it came time to share it with another person because we were afraid of their reaction to hearing the truth about us. The modifications are not intentional efforts to hide the truth; they are more like a knee-jerk reaction to the fear of rejection. It is additionally critical to have a written record of your Sixth Step work as you will continue to benefit from ongoing monitoring of your intervention plans and revisions where indicated.

The art of "quarter turning" (distorting the truth) appears to be second nature to most recovering people. It is not a complicated process and appears to be learned at an early age when we discovered that the twisting of words seemed to lessen a person's reaction to what we were sharing. The process of "quarter turning" is a phrase likened to turning the eyepiece on a microscope slightly in one direction or the other. The movement may appear imperceptible, but the view through the lens is very different. "Quarter turning" results in a level of sharing that is less than honest and the relief one desires from the disclosure is greatly reduced or non-existent. Take, for example, the difference in the following two presentations.

- I was irresponsible with family finances.
- I stole money from the family budget to support my dependency and frequently stole from the children's bank accounts to replace the funds.

Both statements are true, but the first appears less honest than the second one. What is important here is not the vocabulary that is used to share the wrong, but the willingness to relate the exact nature of the wrong. In the second example, the reporter is more likely to experience lasting relief from the disclosure because it accurately communicates the pain he or she felt from the wrong that was committed.

Mentorship

The progression of addiction frequently creates isolation and despair. The loneliness that engulfs the addict and co-addict floods the senses with a perception of uniqueness that often sets the victims apart from help. Sobriety has hopefully moved you from a position of oneness to an acceptance of the community and fellowship available in the 12 Step rooms. Recovery is as much a "we" experience as "active addiction or relapse" is an "I." You never have to recover alone, if you choose. Please take care of your need for support as you move through this soul searching and fact facing process. If you feel the need to talk to a member of your support group or therapist as you pass the searching light of truth over the shadows of your past please take the time to do so. If you do not have a therapist or spiritual advisor contact our offices through www.leademcounseling.com and we will help you find professional support or make arrangements to provide you with a plan to secure distance counseling.

Step-Sponsor Prompts

Step Sponsor Prompts are also introduced throughout your task work to help you remain on track and maximize the use of your time and emotional energy. The prompts are intended to enhance your sense of spirituality or "other centered-ness." Additionally, task specific prompts and exhibits are included along with the explanation of the tasks associated with the Fourth and Sixth Steps.

Stop

Stop prompts you to stop what you are doing. The guide is about to redirect you or offer suggestions that are intended to explain points under review. The time you take examining the points offered can improve the flow of your writing and enhance the depth of your self-exploration. You will not lose your place. The Action prompts will redirect you back to where you left off.

Inner Workings Profile

The Inner Workings Profile prompt signals an opportunity to see what the authors, referred to in the Exhibit under review, were thinking when they prepared the sample entry item. The guide will first provide insight into the authors' thought process and then the actions that were taken. Several examples will be provided to cover the Snapshots that are introduced but they do not cover all the possible interpretations of a particular scene or the feelings that motivated the behavior of the people involved.

Prayer/Meditative Reflection

The Prayer/Meditative Reflection prompts have been inserted at places where you might feel that the work is too challenging or at times when it is thought to be helpful to just reflect on what you have accomplished. The prompt signals an opportunity to become spiritually grounded. You are encouraged to use prayer or meditative reflection to renew your commitment, rest in the safety of the care of your higher power as promised in the Third Step, or draw on the power promised in the Eleventh Step.

Snapshot

The guide is offering an example of how a Task might be completed. It demonstrates what the inventory entry might look like. Two examples are offered reflecting two different depths of exploration styles you can consider. The examples do not have to be followed exactly. Please experiment with a style that works for you. The length of your own entry is not important, just that you accurately describe the experience.

Think

The guide is directing you to think about the Task, questions, or the material presented. You do not need to write anything. You are encouraged, however, to study the Snapshots with an eye on how you can identify with the material presented. If the examples do not have meaning for you then see how you can identify at a feeling level. Remember to identify and not to compare yourself to others. Be mindful that this work can be highly emotional and, as such, greater levels of confusion are possible. Do not be discouraged by the clouds of confusion should they appear. They will pass if you back up from your work and re-read the section that preceded what you are working on or review the inspirational text in Section One. It might also be helpful to review the foundation material provided in our step guides published by Gentle Path Press.

Action

The guide is providing a nudge for you to begin a Task or to return to a Task that you were working on before you were directed to examine supportive materials or take time for self care.

Mentorship

When the Mentorship prompt appears it is intended to serve as a prompt to make contact with a trusted member of your support system to access the insight or support you might be looking for. The form of the contact is up to you. You can phone or arrange for a quick visit if necessary or simply reflect on the time that you have spent together or the inspiration and hope you have experienced through the relationship. If you phone or visit, try to keep it short. You are reaching out for support, encouragement, or the wisdom of another person's experience, strength, and hope and not looking for a way out of the step work.

Time Management

It will be helpful to read the entire guide before beginning any of the suggested tasks but since we seldom follow that suggestion ourselves we encourage you to read the previous chapters when you find yourself bogged down or feeling overwhelmed. Also many clients have found it helpful to study the 12 Step literature produced by the various 12 Step fellowships. Gentle Path Press publishes step guides that provide a much more concentrated study of each of the Steps in a series which the authors are contributors.

The demanding schedules of work, family, home, and recovery can make it difficult to find the time to devote to specific step work. We understand and have found ourselves juggling far too many balls and thinking that the word "balance" should be classified as being a FOUR-letter word of vulgarity. It is important though to make uninterrupted blocks of time available for written step work. The time you invest in this written plan for discovery, accountability, and change will return more rewards from work, family, home, and recovery than it will cost you in lost family or work opportunities. The next chapter will highlight important points to consider before you begin your Fourth Step inventory. It will also promote <u>balance</u>. There we have said it again. Now we will leave you to the work while we wash our mouths out with soap and promise never to use the word again.

Chapter 2: Before the Clearing Begins

The decision to move beyond the maintenance of an abstinent state of being to the development of a sober lifestyle has brought you to this point in your step work. Whether you were encouraged by your support group or prodded by your therapist you have arrived at an acceptance that emotional and spiritual changes will be necessary to accomplish your goal of true emotional sobriety. The authors have come to understand the Fourth through the Seventh Steps as a flowing process of clearing away the wreckage of the past rather than a series of isolated tasks. This guide will help you to understand the relationship that these important steps have to each other and how to capitalize on a new appreciation of their connectivity.

This chapter will: review the steps that precede the cleaning process, introduce suggested pre-requisites to your personal housecleaning, and provide an overview of the process, its purpose, and its benefit to you.

Review of the First Three Steps

The Fourth through the Seventh Steps represent the action steps we undertake to clear away the wreckage of the past life of active addiction and co-addiction that has left a debris field that covered nearly every aspect of our lives. The progression through what were once referred to as the housecleaning steps can sometimes seem quite daunting but do not fear for the authors and many others have made the journey and we will be with you every step of the way.

The 12 Step recovery process that you began in the first three steps can take you from loneliness and desperation to a place of genuine companionship and hope. We hope that you have come to this point in the journey with an appreciation for the many rewards that a life of sobriety makes possible. Before we begin clearing away the wreckage of the past let's take a quick look in the rear view mirror at those important steps.

The first three steps of the twelve-step process of recovery from addictive illnesses read:

1. We admitted we were powerless over (our addictive process) — that our lives had become unmanageable.

2. Came to believe that a Power greater than ourselves could restore us to sanity.

3. Made a decision to turn our will and our lives over to the care of God *as we understood Him.*

Steps 1 - 3 provide the foundation for the development of a way of life that leads the victims of the addiction and co-addiction from a solitary position of "I" to the united reliance on a fellowship of "we." The essential elements of the initial surrender process, which culminates in the Third Step, are summarized in the "ABC's" of recovery as referenced in:

a. That we were alcoholic and could not manage our own lives.

b. That probably no human power could have relieved our alcoholism.

c. That God could and would if He were sought.

The First Step, said to be the only absolute requirement for recovery, requires an admission that your problematic behavior was neither a bad habit nor a cultural difference, but an addiction. The First Step requires an awareness that you did not behave the way that you did when you were active in your addiction and co-addiction because you are Irish, German, uncomfortably short, too fat, young and immature, or because you had an anger management problem. Many of our problematic behaviors were rooted in the progression of our addiction, but not all. Some of our behaviors, as you will learn in the chapters to come, have their foundation in our defects of character.

Your First Step declaration of unmanageability will have required great humility because acceptance of defeat comes painfully slow to most of us. The stories, which described our respective *bottoms*, vary greatly in both the breadth and depth of powerlessness and unmanageability a sufferer will endure before hitting his or her *bottom*. The tasks associated with the completion of a First Step will vary from fellowship to fellowship and sponsor to sponsor. While there is no universally accepted definition of the *bottom*, you will know that you have hit yours by your willingness to acknowledge the need for help outside of yourself. The idea that "probably no human power" will suffice brings the need for further humility in the Second Step.

The Second Step, often overlooked because it is thought to be an extension of the obvious dilemma already addressed in the First Step, is a vital step in the initial surrender process. Many newcomers will miss the implication that will, hopefully, become obvious with time.

> If all of our problems were related to our addiction and the problem was eliminated when we established abstinence, then why would there be a need for a Second Step?

The Second Step is not restating the obvious. It implies that our sanity is not restored merely because we resign ourselves to being powerless. Insanity is often defined as the tendency to do the same things over and over again and expect the results to be different. The unmanageability that re-emerges for those who only establish abstinence is a painful example of this insanity. We need to do more than put the proverbial *cork in the jug*. The alcoholic who stops drinking but continues to romance the good old days and the food addict who avoids forbidden foods but gorges on salad have put the *cork in the jug* but are still behaving like addicts. The recovering sex addict who merely stops the more socially unacceptable aspects of acting out behavior without replacing his or her reliance on external sources of pleasure will eventually find himself or herself *teasing the addiction*. The First Step does not signify or result in surrender. For some it is barely more than a state of resignation to abstinence. The relief obtained from the admission found in the First Step will be short lived if not followed by the pursuit of a Power greater than us. We have a great deal to change about the way that we manage our emotions and interact with others. We will need a power greater than our own to identify and make those changes.

The Third Step can present an ominous challenge to those of us that are still struggling to understand or accept the need for a Power greater than ourselves in recovery. We are told that we cannot maintain sobriety on the Power of our own will. "Will power works about as well on addiction as it does on a <u>bad</u> case of diarrhea," ranted our sponsors. While they preached at us we sometimes thought to ask whether or not there was a "good" case of diarrhea but we thought the wiser of it and chose silence. We, like many, had a great deal to learn about the purpose of a higher power in recovery and even more about how to gain access to that Power.

Whether you believe in God; deny that God's existence is provable; or believe you can prove the non-existence of God; you will need to develop a relationship with a Power greater than yourself. We cannot see ourselves clearly without the help of others and we cannot change what we cannot see. To make matters worse, we appear to be equipped with the ultimate weapon of self-destruction: free will. In the coming steps you will learn much about healthy uses for your willpower but for now it is important to remember that much of our injury has occurred because we are free to do as we please. Your sponsor might joke with you that "your best thinking has gotten you in this mess," but it is hardly a joke. Your thinking will need to change. The way you cope with your emotions will need to change. The way you interrelate with others will need to change. You will find that we are always changing. We are either moving forward or we are moving backward. The choice is yours. This would be a good time to exercise your free will to develop a God of your own understanding. The Power greater than yourself can be your group conscience, a sense of a greater power of the universe, or the collective thinking and wisdom of those you trust. Please do not trust your recovery to yourself alone. We sometimes get defensive when our support group members challenge us to get out of our own heads. It is sound advice because our unchallenged thinking can get us into a great deal of trouble. After all, our thinking occurs in a place where there is no adult supervision.

If you have hit bottom you will have already suffered the lessons you would need to move beyond the First Step to the acceptance of the need for a Power greater than yourself. The first three steps can be simply summed up as: I can't, He can, and I'll let Him. The Third Step did not ask us to relocate ourselves from the pain of active addiction to the oppression of a violent or controlling deity. The Third Step invited us to turn our will and our lives over to the <u>care</u> of God as we understood Him. We will continue to enjoy the comfort of that care as we move through the housecleaning tasks that await us. To be clear about what we mean by housecleaning we will take a more focused look at the concept.

Housecleaning Defined

A housecleaning does not require that the house be demolished. A housecleaning will remove the debris that might make the house less functional, eliminate and or replace items that have outlived their usefulness or have fallen beyond repair, but it will not require a demolition crew. Likewise a decision to clear away the wreckage of the past through your step work does not imply that you are necessarily going to have to change everything about you in order to build the foundation for a sober lifestyle.

There are aspects of our personalities that would be harmless idiosyncrasies or even assets if we would remain abstinent. Newcomers are sometimes teased by those more seasoned members who quip: The only thing you have to change is – everything. While it might be true that we have a great many changes to make, it is not necessarily true that "everything has to go" in order for us to get and remain sober. We do not have to tear ourselves down to build the changes in ourselves that we need to make. The idea that our "best thinking got us in the mess of addiction" is often employed by support group members trying to disarm the challenges of a newcomer to recovery but it should not be assumed that because we are recovering addicts or co-addicts we are incapable of sound reasoning and good choices.

Many of us have core values and belief systems that have been silenced by the progression of our illness and can become a source of personal comfort and strength if given the breadth of sobriety. We may be broken but we are not a mistake. We were not made to be junk even though our behaviors may at times suggest otherwise. You are likely, in fact, to discover or re-discover many of your qualities during your work on the tasks associated with Steps 4 through 7. Leave the wrecking ball of self-condemnation to the demolition crew. We are about construction - not destruction. In case you are not convinced yet, we will highlight what is in it for you.

Why Clean House?

Why, indeed should we clean house? Many of us ask ourselves: "Isn't the past better off left in the past?" Many of us have protested the direction to begin the Fourth Step or refuted the house-cleaning model proposed in this guide with the childlike proposition that we "had changed and knew that we were never going to do it again and that should be enough!" Others offered up other rationalizations with such passion as to leave one thinking that they were quoting the collective wisdom of the ages as justification for dismissing the need to clean house. Our personal favorite pearl of a rationalization has been: "The past is the past, there is nothing you can do to change it – so forget it and move on!" In other words: "Don't cry over spilled milk!" John is really showing his age with that quote.

While we are sure that the idea of promising to never do it again and asking for absolution is a throw back to a childhood strategy of ours, we are suspicious that the latter claim is not a pearl from the collective wisdom of the ages. It sounds more like the self-proclaimed genius of Stosh the bartender at Reilly's Bar and Grill where one of the authors used to sit for hours drinking German beer served by a Polish philosopher (barkeep) at an Irish pub in a passionately Italian neighborhood. Yes, the patron (author) was as fragmented as the advice he received and as contradictory as the setting of the barroom advice preached in isolated recovery meetings. Suffice it to say that the "leave the past in the past" direction was bad advice then and it is bad advice now despite its enduring popularity.

We clean house because we are trying to build anew. We are trying to build a new "us" because the person we were and the philosophical positions we held were leading us to the point of desperation that many of us suffered before getting help. The housecleaning process will help you to sort out what is defective and should be discarded from those aspects of your life that should be preserved and nurtured back into fullness.

What's in It for Me?

Marketing 101 teaches that the consumer needs to understand before the sale what the benefit is going to be. While it is said that the promise of true sobriety should be a source of attraction that does not require promotion, we will provide you with a partial list of possible benefits that are covered in greater detail in *Surveying the Wreckage*, a work by these authors published by Gentle Path Press (2010).

- The *Promises* in *Alcoholics Anonymous*[2] (Alcoholics Anonymous, 1953) that have been reprinted for your reference in the Glossary appear after the Ninth Step. The placement of the *Promises* suggests that they are a part of what is in it for you – if you clean house.
- The feeling memories of the past can haunt you in the form of seething resentments. A housecleaning will begin to drive the "ghosts" away.
- The coping strategies you acquired for dealing with the stories that developed in your past can make it extremely difficult to develop and/or maintain healthy and intimate relationships in the present. If you clean house and develop a comprehensive plan for addressing your defects of character in the Sixth Step you will be able to change your personality.

- You will have an opportunity to develop a comprehensive relapse prevention plan because of the understanding you will develop of the antecedents to many of your current personality defects.
- You will develop your awareness of others and identify ways in which you might participate in the healing of those you have harmed or to promote healing in the lives of those among you who are still suffering.
- The housecleaning process will promote personal congruency. You will learn enough about what you think, how you feel, what you say and how you behave to evolve into ONE you. ONE set of values, ONE standard of behavior, and ONE story to replace the multiple personas that some of us seem to be forced to project.
- A clear view of where you have been is a valuable reference point for future changes. It is not a luxury option of sobriety. It is as much a necessity as a rear view mirror is.
- It will provide vital insights into the rebuilding process that begins in the Eighth Step that will attract others to you and help you to deliver meaningful amends in the Ninth Step.

These benefits and many more will be your reward for your searching and fearless work that awaits you.

Chapter 3: Important Prerequisites to the Housecleaning

This guide is designed to walk you through the tasks associated with the successful completion of Steps 4 through 7, often referred to as the *housecleaning* steps because they make room for a variety of personality and behavioral changes we will need to undertake if we are truly ready to experience the *Promises* of sober living. While there are no mandatory pre-requisites to undertaking this housecleaning it is advisable that you begin the journey with a solid emotional and spiritual foundation. The elements that you may find useful in building that foundation include:

- Establishment of a period of abstinence from your *drug of choice* sufficient to allow you the opportunity to successfully manage the withdrawal associated with your illness without relapse
- Development of a clear understanding of the symptoms of your illness that are particular to your story
- Organization of the elements of your story that reflect both the powerlessness and unmanageability in your life associated with your addictive illness
- Production and delivery of an honest disclosure of your First Step to the intimate members of your support group
- Freedom from the use of any addictive substance regardless of whether or not you view yourself as having a history of substance related addiction
- Development and maintenance of a working relationship with a Power greater than yourself from which or whom you derive comfort and support
- Establishment of the foundation for an intimate, reliable, and objective support system (which includes a sponsor) and whose members share their own struggles with recovery as they are helping to guide you through yours
- Confirmation that you are not considered by anyone (including yourself) to be dangerous to yourself or others
- Clear articulation to your significant others and your support group about the potentially distressing step work you are about to begin
- Established membership in a 12 Step group which includes: the practice of regular attendance at 12 Step meetings, active participation in the activities of your home group, and the maintenance of a plan for conducting "12 Step " work in the recovery community
- Mindfulness of the potential impact of your emotional reactivity on those around you during the process of completing these steps
- Maintenance of a plan for daily prayer and meditation
- Establishment of a communicated plan for ensuring undisturbed blocks of time to complete the task work involved in these steps

Step-Sponsor Prompt

Mentorship

Before you begin your written work on the Tasks for completing Component 1 of your Fourth Step inventory take the time to review the above points with your sponsor, your therapist, or members of your support group.

Section 2: Putting an End to the Secrets - Steps 4 & 5

Chapter 1: Examining the Wreckage

The tasks we have prepared for completing your Fourth Step are intended to support (rather than replace) the recovery efforts you have already undertaken in your relationships with members of your support group and in your growing relationship with a "higher power."

This guide is offered as a resource for the universe of people engaged in recovery from the tragedy of an addictive illness whether the costs you endured were in your role as an addict or that of a co-addict. The examples given throughout the guide are offered as a small sample of the possible behavioral manifestations to be found in the various addictive disorders. It is fortunate that, while our symptoms might be different, the progressive nature of the illness we share is a common bond. The 12 Steps of Alcoholics Anonymous[2] have been adopted by over 50 self-help fellowships and the number is climbing every year. This guide can be easily adapted to accept the symptoms you bring to the Fourth Step experience, but is not intended to offer examples that are specific to every addictive illness. You are invited to contact us at www.leademcounseling.com if you have difficulty making the adaptations you need to adequately address your particular recovery needs. In spite of the frequent references to God, this meditation course is meant for people of all spiritual affiliations – religious, a-religious, agnostic, and atheist. Please understand the use of God is to suggest the God of your understanding or your higher power. Likewise, the daily prayer is meant to help with spiritual grounding. A meditative scene or fond memory can be just as helpful.

Additionally it is important to note that many of the 12 Step fellowships offer printed material that can help you in the process of adapting our model to your specific recovery plan. Many of the citations in this guide will direct your attention to the material first published by Alcoholics Anonymous[2] because the organization is the grandparent of all 12 Step groups (and not because it holds the market on recovery wisdom). An effort to include even a small cross section of the available 12 Step recovery literature would be exhausting and the writings of many other fellowships would still be ignored. We encourage you to build your own library of recovery materials and avoid limiting yourself to any one philosophical or psychological school of thought. The nation's libraries and bookstores maintain a treasure trove of resources to help you to develop the interpersonal skills you will need to establish and maintain freedom from your addictive illness. We hope this guide will take a place among other heavily used works in your personal library.

The journey that you are about to embark on can seem quite threatening, but innumerable recovering people before you have traveled it without peril. Those who stumble seem to be those who avoid these vital steps. Those who complete their inventory with thoroughness and honesty, withholding nothing, report that they feel a closer relationship with their higher power and a faith in their ability to change the self-destructive patterns of behavior that had deprived them of true sobriety.

Our own initial experiences with the Fourth Step were painfully unfulfilling. We learned little about the patterns of our behavior and nothing about how to avoid repeating the same self-defeating actions. We left our first Fifth Step experiences feeling disappointed and with many of the same resentments and feelings of self-recrimination that we had before we began. Subsequent Fourth Step attempts produced little more than a brief period of relief. We had consulted many "old timers" in search of the "right" way to complete a searching and fearless moral inventory and accumulated over a dozen guides with which we experimented, but the results were equally unrewarding.

We used questionnaires that appeared to ask every question imaginable, yet generated little more than a well-organized history. We tried using a model built on a table formatting to identify cause and effect relationships between our behavior and our resentments, but we were unsuccessful. Generally, this approach resulted in a superficial assessment of problems that represented serious flaws in our character. These personality traits would need closer examination for they had delivered a devastating impact on our lives and the lives of those around us. We suspected that the effort of merely outlining our resentments would yield only marginal results, and we were right. The problem had not been the particular models we had chosen, for they had worked for other people. The models simply did not match us.

Our personality was not any more complicated than that of the typical person in recovery. We were not unique; we were just different. We later came to believe that our personality in general and our coping strategies in particular were shaped by the feeling experiences we had accumulated. The tables, questionnaires, and outlines we experimented with left us confused and without focus or clear direction. We were not linear learners. We were experience-based learners and would need to use a format that would guide us through our feeling experiences. The guide that we have prepared for you evolved through the trial and error that we tolerated to get to the point at which we could understand how to examine our "stock-in-trade."

The format is simple, but the process is intensely probing. We learned to use our feeling memory rather than our thinking memory to guide us to the patterns of our past. The injuries we endured were revealed to us in a way that allowed us to recognize self-defeating thinking and behavior patterns which had escaped us in previous inventory attempts.

Overview of the Four Components of a Comprehensive Fourth Step

The components have been taken from a summary of the Fourth Step process found in *Alcoholics Anonymous*[2] (1953) on page 70. It is reprinted here for your reference:

> "If we have been thorough about our personal inventory, we have written down a lot. We have listed and analyzed our resentments. We have begun to comprehend their futility and their fatality. We have commenced to see their terrible destructiveness. We have begun to learn tolerance, patience and good will toward all men, even our enemies, for we look on them as sick people. We have listed the people we have hurt by our conduct, and are willing to straighten out the past if we can."

Each of the four components identified in the summary above contribute to what is described as being the usual elements of a "thorough … and … personal inventory." The first two components of a personal inventory, as used in this guide are taken from the line: "We have listed and analyzed our resentments." The first 164 pages of *Alcoholics Anonymous*[2] (1953), provide a vast amount of information regarding the strategies for identifying resentments, the threat they pose to the recovery process, and methods for analyzing and resolving resentments. They should be studied and not merely read because they are written as a recovery text. The third and fourth components of a personal inventory are introduced in the last sentence of this condensed explanation: "We have listed the people we have hurt by our conduct, and are willing to straighten out the past if we can."

In the pages to come, this guide will provide a detailed explanation of each component and samples that demonstrate an effective way to proceed through your inventory. Your movement through the four components will be difficult at times because they cover the fullness of your life and the emotional exhaustion can make the journey appear unbearable. It is not. You may decide to concentrate for a period of time on a single component rather than push through all four but please do not get stuck in negative projection. You will get through them all one component at a time.

Before we begin with the first component we want to provide you with an overview of all four components to completing a searching and fearless moral inventory as developed in this guide.

Inventory Components: An Overview

List Our Resentments (Component 1)

The first component of the inventory will ask you to write a great deal about the ways in which you have been wronged by other people and institutions in your life. The format for the component is explained in further detail in the coming pages. The guide will request that you examine your recent and past experiences to identify the ways you have been harmed, and the feelings and resentments that have accompanied those harms.

The process of listing all of the harms can be quite exhausting, but thoroughness is the key to your success in this step. Many folks have complained that the act of writing out the wrongs that are repeated many times over by the same person are an unnecessary waste of time. We assure you that it will be energy well spent when it comes time to read your inventory during your Fifth Step experience. The writing activity will seem like unneeded repetition until you hear yourself share what you have written with the human recipient of your Fifth Step. During the reading, you will get a powerful understanding of the depth and extent of injury you have been exposed to and the coping strategies that developed within your personality to respond to those harms. If you are thorough in your effort, withholding nothing and presenting the material in exact terms, you will gain valuable insight into your defects of character and the ways in which they have dulled the joy in your life. The insights you obtain will answer questions like: "Why do I keep picking partners who are emotionally unavailable?"

Analyze Our Resentments (Component 2)

The second component deals with the analysis of your resentments and will present a series of questions which will help you to identify patterns in the behaviors of others which have caused you harm. It will also help you gain insight into the personalities of those who have harmed you so you can better understand how to shield yourself from similar or continued harm in the future.

The questions are offered as a guide and it is not necessary to answer any of them. You may decide to select those questions that focus on issues that you would like to explore further. If you decide to use the questions presented, they can guide your reflections and help you to analyze your resentments in a way that will enable you to develop strategies for addressing them. You can write your responses to the questions you choose and share them in your Fifth Step or with a sponsor at some later date. You may also answer the questions silently to yourself through your own thoughtful reflections.

List Our Wrongs (Component 3)

The third component of the inventory, like the first, may require a great deal of writing. The Tasks will ask you to examine, in detail, the wrongs that you have committed against the people or institutions in your life. The format for this component is explained in detail in the pages to come. The guide will request that you examine your recent and past experiences to identify the ways in which you have harmed others. You will be encouraged to explore in further detail how your behavior toward others has affected your life. Your thoroughness will be rewarded when it comes time to complete your Sixth and Seventh Steps because you will have gained new insights into the self-defeating patterns of your own behavior and enable you to replace the behaviors associated with your defects of character with healthy coping strategies.

It is important that you include those wrongs that were never discovered by others. The fact that the victims did not know that you committed the wrong has not taken away the guilt, shame, and remorse you have been feeling.

Straighten out the Past if We Can (Component 4)

Many of us begin our inventory with a focus on our desire to clear away the wreckage of the past. In many cases, our willingness to address the brokenness of our interpersonal relationships is strong because we are able to see that the people who we still care for have been hurt. In some cases, we have attempted to maintain our relationships with these people, especially in the cases of family members and long-time friends.

If we are sincere about our desire to practice the principles of recovery in all of our affairs, this fourth component of the inventory is the beginning of the amends process that will be developed further in Steps 8 and 9 of your respective fellowship. In the fourth component you will be asked to examine the type of relationship you would like to have with each of the living persons on your Master List of resentments that you will be creating in the tasks ahead. Questions will be offered to aid you in your reflection. Within the guide you will find prompts that are intended to alert you to important points or to give specialized instruction.

Step-Sponsor Prompt

Think

Before you begin your written work on the Tasks let us read and review all 10 Tasks for completing Component 1 of your Fourth Step inventory.

Tasks Associated with Component 1

The guide uses ten specific and measureable tasks that guide you through the process of completing Component 1 of your Fourth Step. They are listed here as an introduction for future reference:

1. Create a Master List of every person or institution that has ever wronged you.

2. Create a separate Title Page for each person or institution you have identified on the Master List and place the name of each person or institution on the top of his or her own page.

3. Place the stack of Title pages in front of you and choose which person or institution to begin with.

4. On the Title Page, for the person or institution you have chosen to describe, write in detail one of the wrongs that person or institution has done to you.

5. The guide is designed to use your feeling memories to identify other similar life experiences. Your reflections on the following two questions will remind you of the other people or institutions which have harmed you.

    When have I felt this way?

    Who else has treated me this way?

6. Look at your Master List and identify the people or institutions that have harmed you in a similar fashion. If your reflections on the questions in Task 5 brought new people or institutions to mind, add them to the Master List and give them their own page.

7. Pull out the pages for each of the people or institutions that came to mind in Task 5. Once again, identify and describe the wrong that each person or institution did to you, as you did in Task 4.

8. When you complete each of entries for the additional people or institutions, place their pages back in the unfinished pile.

9. Pull the first page back out and continue with the next wrong for that person as you did in Task 4. Each time you add a new wrong for this person or institution, complete Tasks 5, 6, and 7.

10. When you are finished moving back and forth among the various people or institutions, you are finished with Component 1.

Chapter 2: Component 1 - List Our Resentments

It is time to begin developing your inventory. This chapter introduces the first component of the inventory that addresses the wrongs and injuries you have suffered. The Tasks will direct you to move back and forth between the various experiences that have had a negative impact on your life. The Task items, which are marked 1 through 10, will ask you to consider the ways that you have been harmed and the similarities of the wrongs that you have endured in your life. Your feeling memories will lead you from one time of your life to another and one situation to another. Do not worry about keeping them in chronological order. This is not an essay. You are creating a picture of your life to review with God and another human being in your Fifth Step. It does not have to follow a particular order and there are no right answers. The only absolute is that you be honest and thorough.

Your spirit will be deeply challenged by waves of strong emotions. Let them come. The past will not overwhelm you if you embrace it. The only power the "past" has is the power it gains from secrecy and denial. If we share the past, it loses its power. Remember the old saying: We are only as sober as our deepest, darkest secrets!

When describing the wrongs that you have endured at the hands of others avoid the inclination to minimize the impact of the wrong. This is an appropriate time to establish a written validation of the accounts of your injuries. Do not rationalize why a wrong was committed and at all costs avoid justifying the wrongs of others as being related to some behavior of yours. There will be time in Component 2 to understand why people may have treated you the way they did. Component 3 will ask you to examine the harms you have caused others. This is not the place to write about what you did. Focus your attention on the behaviors of others and how you were hurt. You may not be able to overcome your resentments or could find that old resentments resurface in the future if you co-mingle the wrongs that you have endured with those you have caused.

Step-Sponsor Prompts

Prayer

God, help me to remain focused on the task at hand. You know my heart and can see my desire to bring my past into perspective. I want to learn from my past, not live in it. I pray that you give me courage when fear and pride rear their ugly heads to taunt me into giving up on myself. Reveal to me those life experiences that have helped to shape my personality for there is much repair work to be done.

Meditative Reflection

Sit quietly for a moment longer and imagine yourself in a safe place where you are free of the torment of the past and the dread of the future. Smell the freedom. Taste the crisp air of clarity that lies ahead. Embrace the hope you have acquired as you have watched others get well. Allow yourself to rest in the knowledge that the power you were given in the Third Step can be drawn on any time you need it.

Mentorship

Take a moment to reflect on what you have already accomplished in your recovery efforts with your sponsor or other members of your support group. Picture some of the time that you have spent with these people and the hope that you drew from those experiences. Feel free to place a call to one of them for support if you need it. If available get a hug from a family member who understands the nature of the journey that you are on.

Action

The 10 Tasks may seem overwhelming at first but you will quickly become familiar with the feeling flow that they create. Your feeling memories will provide you with many sensations that will direct you to scenes in your life that you will need to write about. If you keep your focus on this inventory being a journey that leads to the freedom that comes from self awareness and emotional relief you will not experience it as an endurance contest. If you are ready, let us go to work on the Tasks! You might want to remove Appendix B from the back of the guide and place it along side of you as you work.

It is time to begin your writing on the Tasks associated with Component 1 - List Our Resentments. Work will begin with Task 1.

~ Task 1 ~

Create a Master List of every person or institution that has ever wronged you.

You will want to keep your Master List handy because you will probably add people or institutions to it as you complete the 10 numbered Tasks for this Component. When you are developing your list, do not exclude people merely because they have also been hurt by you or because you believe that they were only paying you back for the hurt they felt. You will cover your wrongs later. Do not concern yourself with keeping the list of the offenders in chronological order or with ordering them in terms of the degree of hurt you have endured. Neither formula for ordering the list is required. Simply list the people or institutions that have caused you harm as they occur to you.

Avoid the tendency to exclude someone from your list because you do not believe that listing them is fair. Here is a collection of some INVALID reasons for excluding someone or some institution from the master list for Component 1 - Task 1:

- The person did not mean it
- The person was injured a great deal in his or her own life
- The person did not know any better
- The person did the best job that he or she could
- I have already forgiven the person
- I don't need to address him or her because I have done the same things to them or others
- I should not focus on the harms he or she caused because I know that he or she really loved me
- I had it coming to me

- He or she was just doing what they knew
- I do not even have proof that he or she did it
- I do not believe that it was really his or her intention to hurt me

There are many other <u>seemingly</u> legitimate reasons for excluding someone from the list but there is no excusing hurtful behavior. The harms you experienced were real if they felt real regardless of whatever else you know about the person, the circumstances, or possible motivations. You will explore all those issues further in Component 2.

Step-Sponsor Prompt

Mentorship

If you are having difficulty identifying people or institutions that belong on this Master List you might get a jump start by conferring with your sponsor, therapist, family member, or support group member. It is likely that they will remember your having made past references to harms that you have endured at the hands of others. It might also be helpful to peruse an old photo album, as it will stir your memories.

~ Task 2 ~

Create a separate Title Page for each person or institution you have identified on the Master List and place the name of each person or institution on the top of his or her own Title Page.

You will probably need numerous sheets so have a supply handy. It might be easier to keep track of your work if you use loose-leaf sheets of paper because there are likely to be corrections that will become messy if you try to use a bound notebook whose pages are not easily detachable. Clip a few blank sheets to the Title Page for each person so you do not have to stop the flow of your writing to find extra paper when you are working. You will end up with quite a few individual pages, so you might want to number the pages belonging to each person or institution on the Master List so you do not lose track and keep them in a folder marked Component 1 - List Our Resentments.

You will prepare a Title Page for each person on your list even if you do not yet know what it is that you want to write about. If the person or institution comes to mind as being a source of harm in your life then create a Title Page for that person or institution. Your entries should be numbered for each person and you will begin your written work on the Title Page for that person or institution you chose to begin with. Before you continue onto Component 1 - Task 3 double-check your Master List to be sure that you have a Title Page for each person.

~ Task 3 ~

Place the stack of Title Pages in front of you and choose which person or institution to begin with.

It does not matter which person or institution you choose to begin with. Upcoming Tasks will direct you to consider the harms you have endured from other people or institutions that are similar to the ones experienced with the person you first choose to write about. You can pick the person that you are currently the closest to or select a person that has had minimal impact on your life.

Step-Sponsor Prompt

Think

In Task 4 you will be asked to begin describing the hurts that you have suffered in individual inventory entries. Before beginning, let us stop for a moment and examine the differences between a productive and an unproductive inventory entry. It is easy to become confused when writing about the wrongs other people or institutions have done to you. It is common to want to make excuses for other's hurtful behavior as a way of numbing the pain you feel. If you are still involved with the person or institution, you might also want to explain away the harm to make your continued involvement with the person or institution tolerable. Throughout the guide you will be referred to productive and unproductive sample entries to help with your writing. Spend time reading through the descriptions for productive and unproductive entries and study the Exhibits offered before continuing on with Component 1 – Task 4.

Productive Entries

Productive Entries are those that keep the focus on what happened and what was felt rather than attempting to explain the reason why something occurred. In the written entries for Component 1 (List My Resentments) and Component 3 (List My Wrongs) you are not being asked to explain the reason for the behavior that is described. Productive entries answer the following questions:

- What was the setting in which the wrong occurred?
- What were the specific details of the wrong by which you were injured?
- Who was present?
- How did others and I feel at the time?
- What impact has the event had on my life since?

Unproductive Entries

Unproductive Entries often include all the facts, but the writer's focus is misguided and the spirit of the Task is ignored. Unproductive examples are offered in the guide to show what it looks like when you lose focus. This loss of focus occurs when the writer: makes excuses for the wrongs that have been committed; minimizes the wrong by rationalizing or blaming others; and/or tries to establish arguments that a particular wrong is merely a reaction to someone else's behavior, thereby lessening the responsibility of the person or institution who committed the wrong.

Step-Sponsor Prompt

Snapshot

Here are two snapshots that show productive entries that clearly focus on the wrongs that the writer endured. Exhibit 1 is an example of a wrong done by a person. Exhibit 2 is an example of a wrong done by an institution. Following each example is an Inner Workings Profile to help illustrate what the author was thinking during the preparation of the sample entries. The feelings associated with each event are <u>underlined</u> for future reference.

Exhibit: 1
Title: Dad
Subtitle: Productive Entry

When I was ten years old, I was <u>fearfully</u> awaiting my Dad's arrival at my Boy Scout promotion ceremony where I was going to receive several merit badges. Mom was there, but all the other guys had both of their parents flanking them and they were beaming with pride. My Mom looked nervous. I felt like I was going to be <u>sick (fear)</u>. The ceremony began without my Dad and I was really <u>hurt</u>. I was not surprised though because he never showed for anything. Before I could clear my head of that thought, Dad staggered into the ceremony room and fell on the floor drunk. I was so <u>mortified</u>. I could not catch my breath. My friend Bob and all the guys stared, waiting to see what was going to happen next. The adults began to whisper to each other and Mom began to cry. I left that night in <u>shame</u> while Bob giggled. I was angry with myself for having invited him. There would be no merit badges and no more scouting because I could never show my face in there again. Dad had ruined that the way he ruined everything. Since then, I have often thought of the public <u>humiliation</u> that I suffered that summer. I learned that night I could not count on anyone but myself and I would spend many years unwilling to trust others or my own feelings. I was so <u>angry</u>. How could I have been so <u>stupid</u> as to believe that he cared enough about me to not drink that night?

Step-Sponsor Prompt

Inner Workings Profile

Exhibit 2 will give you an opportunity to see what the author was thinking when he prepared the Productive Entry you just read.

Exhibit: 2
Title: Dad
Subtitle: Productive Entry

Thought process

The author reflects back on the times in his life when he has felt hurt and remembers a time in the Boy Scouts when he was really hurt by his Dad.

Actions

The author describes the setting:

Ten years old at a Boy Scout ceremony.

The author describes the specific details associated with the wrong:

The author was expecting his parents to share in the celebration of his scouting accomplishments but, instead, his father showed up drunk and humiliated him.

The author identifies the key people present at the time of his injury:

The author identifies his Dad, Mom, and friend Bob as being key participants.

The author identifies and underlines the feelings that he and others were experiencing:

Feelings of fear, sickness, nervousness, hurt, humiliation, mortification, shame, anger, and stupidity.

The author describes the impact the event had on him at the time and since then:

He described his decision to leave the Scouts. The future impact was shown in the difficulty he had trusting people in the future.

Step-Sponsor Prompt

Snapshot

Exhibit 3 will present an example of a Productive Entry on an injury experienced with an institution.

Exhibit: 3
Title: The Phone Company
Subtitle: Productive Entry

Approximately two years ago, we began experiencing problems on our phone line that, at first, were just annoying, but eventually became the focus of an <u>enraged</u> feud. The disruption to our business because of the downtime generated a significant loss of income because we were unable to take orders for merchandise from our catalog. The phone company representative did not seem interested in our complaints and claimed no responsibility for our loss of income, refusing to reduce our bill for the period of seven days of lost service. I felt <u>angry</u> and <u>impotent</u> at the time because there was nothing we could do to appeal the issue to an impartial judge. The <u>powerlessness</u> I felt was a strong reminder of the years of <u>weakness</u> I felt growing up in my alcoholic home. I find myself still quite <u>angry</u> with the phone company and cringe with <u>bitterness</u> when I hear a commercial or see an advertisement of theirs. I am thinking of expanding our business, but the expansion would increase our dependence on the existing phone service. I am too <u>angry</u> and <u>fearful</u> to make a move.

Step-Sponsor Prompt

Inner Workings Profile

Exhibit 4 will give you an opportunity to see what the author was thinking when he prepared the Productive Entry you just read.

Exhibit: 4
Title: The Phone Company
Subtitle: Productive Entry

Thought Process

The author reflects back on the institutions that he believes have treated him unfairly. He quickly focuses on an incident that developed two years ago but which was still very fresh in his mind.

Actions

The author describes the setting:

Two years ago a series of angry phone arguments developed over a service complaint with the phone company.

The author describes the specific details associated with the wrong:

The author's business phone service had been poorly managed for approximately two years and the disruption to business generated a significant loss of income because he was unable to take orders for merchandise from his business catalog.

He identifies the key people present at the time of his injury:

The phone company representative.

He identifies and underlines the feelings that he and others were experiencing:

Feelings of rage, anger, impotence, powerlessness, weakness, bitterness, and fear.

He describes the impact the event had on him at the time and since then:

At the time of the incident we suffered financial loss and emotional stress. The lingering resentment continues to threaten the future growth of the business.

Step-Sponsor Prompts

Think

As you are describing the wrongs that the person or institution has committed, avoid making excuses for their behavior. It is especially important that you do not include your wrong or your part in the harm - if there was one - for it will only diminish the feelings that are important to have validated. A clear understanding of those feelings of harm will be important in order for you to complete Component 2. For example, it is not productive to write: "My father would beat me because I was a bad child." If you were a bad child, you can write about it later in Component 3 when you examine your wrongs. For right now, stick to how you were harmed. All too often this point is missed and we excuse the wrongs others have done by saying, "I guess they did the best job they could," only to find years later that the resentment had not been resolved or removed. The resentment will begin to fade in Component 2 and during your Fifth Step, but a lasting relief will require an intensive effort in the practice of your Sixth and Seventh Steps that will be covered later in this guide.

Snapshot

The following Unproductive Entry (Exhibit 5) will give you an opportunity to see what happens when an inventory author loses focus and misses the spirit of the Task. The Unproductive Entry on the next page uses the same facts that were illustrated in the Snapshot on Dad in Exhibit 1. The Unproductive Entry dilutes and minimizes the wrong that was committed through the use of rationalizing and emotional blocking. The statements that make the entry unproductive have been bolded to highlight them. Following the Unproductive Entry, you will find a Step-Sponsor Prompt - Inner Workings Profile (Exhibit 6).

Exhibit: 5
Title: Dad
Subtitle: Unproductive Entry

When I was ten years old, I was <u>fearfully</u> awaiting my Dad's arrival at my Boy Scout promotion ceremony where I was going to receive several merit badges. Mom was there, but all the other guys had both of their parents flanking them and they were beaming with pride. My mom looked nervous. I felt like I was going to be <u>sick</u>. The ceremony began without my Dad and I was really hurt. It was not a surprise though, because he never showed for anything. **Mom always said that Dad did not attend my functions because he had to work overtime, so I thought he might have been stuck at the plant. I was hoping he had some great excuse.**

Before I could clear my head of that thought, Dad staggered into the ceremony room and fell on the floor, drunk. I was so <u>mortified</u> I could not catch my breath. **Mom whispered that it would be all right. She said that Dad's drinking was a weakness he developed in the war and that I should accept him the way he is and I felt <u>guilty.</u>** All the guys were waiting to see what was going to happen next. The adults began to whisper to each other and Mom began to cry. I left that night in <u>shame</u> while my friend Bob giggled. I was <u>angry</u> with myself for ever having invited Dad. **When was I ever going to learn my lesson? I was never satisfied as a kid. I always wanted more out of people. If only I could have learned to lower my expectations of people, I would not have been <u>hurt.</u>** There would be no merit badges and no more Scouts because I could never show my face in there again. Dad had ruined that the same way he ruined everything **but I had it coming because I was <u>stupid</u>.** Since then, I have often thought of the public <u>humiliation</u> that I suffered that summer. I learned that night I could not count on anyone but myself and I would spend many years unwilling to trust others or my own feelings.

I was so <u>angry</u>. How could I have been so stupid to believe that he cared enough to refrain from drinking that night? I had learned the hard way that you could not count on others for anything. **I had been <u>stupid</u> for trusting. Mom said I should be grateful that he showed up at all. I guess she was right. I should have been able to see that he really loved me by the effort he put into getting there.**

Step-Sponsor Prompt

Inner Workings Profile

Exhibit 6 will give you an opportunity to see what the author was thinking when he prepared the Unproductive Entry you just reviewed in Exhibit 5. This is presented as an Unproductive Entry because the author had been genuinely injured by the experience but he is not giving himself the permission to feel uncomfortable. His denial system as a co-addicted child growing up in an alcoholic home is well developed and he is likely to have a longstanding pattern of letting people off the hook because he is too uncomfortable to address the hurt involved. He is likely to continue being resentful of his father and other people that remind him of the people in attendance at the event. The Productive Entry enables him to work on the emotional baggage that he is left with. This Unproductive Entry will cause him to stuff his emotions further down. The stuffing will cause either an implosion or an explosion at a later date.

Exhibit: 6
Title: Dad
Subtitle: Unproductive Entry

Thought Process

The author reflects back on the times in his life when he has felt hurt:

He remembers a time in the Boy Scouts when he was really hurt by his Dad. The author has a tendency to become deeply conflicted when he recalls times in his life when loved ones have hurt him. His usual pattern is to initially become angry with the person who was harming him. He gets uncomfortable with the anger or feels disloyal and he begins making excuses for the people who treated him poorly.

Actions

The author describes the setting:

Ten years old at a Boy Scout ceremony.

He describes the specific details associated with the wrong:

The author was expecting his parents to share in the celebration of his scouting accomplishments and instead his father showed up drunk. The author's mother begins to make excuses for his father's behavior and attempts to guilt the author into avoiding judgment of his father or is attempting to prevent the author from reacting in the scene.

He identifies the key people present at the time of his injury:

The author identifies his Dad, Mom, and his friend Bob as the key participants.

He identifies and underlines the feelings that he and others were experiencing:

Feelings of fear, sickness, hurt, mortification, guilt, shame, humiliation, anger, and stupidity.

The author makes excuses for Dad's behavior:

Dad was probably working late and Dad's drinking is a bad habit that he acquired in the war and that should excuse his father's hurtful behavior (rationalization). He blames himself for the hurt that he experienced. He was angry with himself for having invited his Dad in the first place, but he blocked the anger and hurt by saying that he "should have been able to see" that his Dad really loved him (emotional blocking). He blames himself because his own expectations are too high.

Step-Sponsor Prompts

Think

The Unproductive Entry illustrated in Exhibit 5 does not result in a housecleaning as expected. The entry is likely to leave the author confused, unhappy, and unfulfilled. When this entry is delivered in the author's Fifth Step, it is not likely that he will experience the relief that is promised. It might be a good idea to review the Productive Entry (Exhibit 1) again so you can appreciate the differences between two different accounts of the same event.

Prayer

Take a moment to ground yourself with prayer and meditation. While we have provided only a small sample of the type of injuries that twelve steppers face in recovery these examples may have begun to stir emotions in you because of your identification. That is what is expected. You may find yourself wandering off a task you are addressing for one person because it triggers painful memories of other experiences. Take this pause to refresh yourself.

God, help me to maintain the courage I was given when I began this inventory. I am somewhat overloaded with the amount of work I have undertaken in this guide. Help me to acknowledge the truth about myself and the truth about the people who have touched my life.

Meditative Reflection

Focus on the location in which you will deliver your Fifth Step. Focus on your sponsor nodding his or her head with encouragement as you deliver the final entries in your inventory. Feel the sense of accomplishment that will come with the conclusion of a thorough housecleaning. See yourself feeling tired, but strong and able to face life's challenges with pride and humility. You have cleared away some of the wreckage of a lifetime and will now be able to rebuild.

Think

Let us take a moment to review what you have done so far before you begin writing about the wrongs that you have endured.

Thus far you have:

- Created a Master List of all the people and institutions that you have felt harmed by in Task 1
- Created a separate Title Page for each person or institution you identified on the Master List and placed the name of each person or institution on the top of their own page in Task 2
- Placed the stack of Title Pages in front of you and chose which person or institution to begin with in Task 3
- Read through the description of Task 4
- Examined the Snapshot examples of Productive and Unproductive Entries in Exhibits 1, 3, and 5 to better understand the differences between the two so you can avoid using Unproductive Entries that fail to produce the desired relief
- Examined the Inner Workings Profile in Exhibits 2, 4, and 6 to develop insight into the thoughts and actions of the author when he created the Productive and Unproductive Entries
- Spent time in prayer and meditative reflection to get emotionally grounded and spiritually centered

Mentorship

If you have historically had difficulty getting your thoughts and feelings on paper, this next Task could increase your writer's block. Many people have gotten over this obstacle through the use of a scribe. You could use a willing friend or loved one to create rough drafts of your responses to Tasks that require writing and you can edit them later.

The material that you are dictating should not involve your scribe or contain information that your scribe might become distressed over. Make sure you have reviewed these two concerns with prospective volunteers. Also be careful to avoid having your scribe decide what you were thinking or feeling about the events or people in question.

Action

We are resuming here at Task 4. Let us get back to work. It is time to begin the hard stuff.

~ Task 4 ~

On the Title Page for the person or institution you have chosen to begin with, describe in detail one of the wrongs that person or institution has done to you.

If you get stuck, refer back to the Productive and Unproductive Entries shown earlier in Exhibits 1, 3, and 5. In your description, include an approximation of when the wrong occurred, what the setting was, who the participants were, exactly what the wrong was, and how you were injured. Each time you complete a description of a wrong in Task 4 try to describe the feelings, both past and present, which are associated with the wrong.

Step-Sponsor Prompt

Think

Please describe only one event at a time. Now you are thinking, "I will be writing for weeks. This is crazy." You are right. You will be writing a lot. We have described the need for written accountability and thoroughness at great length but let us remind you again that everything you are writing about has actually injured you and that fact warrants validating your injuries in writing.

The following two questions might be helpful for you to consider once you have described the facts:

How did the wrong make me feel at the time?

Describe your feeling reaction in as much detail as you are capable. If you are having a hard time naming your feelings, you can use "comfortable" or "uncomfortable" or see Appendix F for a list of feeling words that you can use.

How has the wrong affected my life since?

This question is asking that you look at the ways in which you believe you have suffered from the harm since the event that it occurred in. We are not encouraging you to blame others for the quality of your life today. We are asking you to consider that some of the harms done to you have had a lasting impact on you that you might not always be aware of. Many of the harms we experienced in the past have a habit of coming back to haunt us in our recovery. We often find people retaliating in the present with a loved one for harms done in the past by a different person. You may have already explored this issue with a sponsor or a spiritual advisor to your satisfaction, but it is important that you persist. You will be deeply moved by the amount of injury that you have suffered and the sharing of that pain in your Fifth Step will result in great relief.

You do not need proof that the harm has been committed. You only need to believe that it did through your feeling or perception of the event in question.

Step-Sponsor Prompts

Stop

Before you move on to the next harm that the person or institution caused you, complete Tasks 5 and 6. These Tasks will not require you to write anything. You will only need an open mind and heart. Let your feelings be your guide. You will come back to the original person when you are finished identifying other harms.

Action

Let's continue with Task 5. You will be using your feeling memories to identify other similar life experiences. Remember that your are not required to have visual proof of a harm endured or a complete recollection of all of the particulars of an event.

~ Task 5 ~

The guide is designed to use your feeling memories to identify other similar life experiences. Your reflections on the following two questions will remind you of the other people or institutions you have been harmed by. Consider the following questions:

When else have I felt this way?
Who else has treated me this way?

Your reflections on the above two questions will remind you of the other people or institutions you have been harmed by. This is important because oftentimes the injury we feel from one person's wrong triggers our feeling memory of all the other hurts we have endured. In addition, it is common for us to overreact to the wrong that is done by someone today because of all the hurts we have collected from others in the past. This Task will help bring those insights into your awareness and make it easier for you to detect when you are overreacting in the future.

We have often found ourselves in the present time asking, "Why did I react so wildly to what another person said or did?" We think to ourselves: "That person did not deserve my reaction based on what he or she did or said." We overreact in present situations to people or their behavior because of unresolved resentments from past times when we have been treated in similar ways by others. Contrary to what many of us would like to believe, the past is not forgotten just because we have tried to will it away. Talk to anyone who has relapsed and they will tell you how quickly past resentments surfaced when they returned to their *drug of choice*. Resentments cannot be willed away. God will remove them if we are doing the step work. So get back to work!

Step-Sponsor Prompts

Mentorship

You might want to rest a bit before continuing on because this depth of self-examination can be emotionally and physically tiring. Call your sponsor or talk to a support group member about how you are feeling. If you are going to take a nap arrange with someone to help you remain accountable to return to your work.

Think

Think for a moment or two about all that you have to be grateful for in your recovery. Stroke yourself for the commitment that you have made to complete your inventory and share your gratitude with the God of your understanding before getting back to work on Component 1 – Task 4. Avoid looking ahead at how many tasks you have left as it might discourage you (24 Tasks remaining for your Fourth Step). Please excuse John, he is such a child and he cannot count either – there are only 23!

∼ Task 6 ∼

After reflecting on the questions in Task 5 look at your Master List and identify the people or institutions that have harmed you in a similar fashion. If your reflections on the two questions in Task 5 brought new people or institutions to mind, add them to the Master List and give them each their own Title Page.

The size of your Master List is likely to grow and as it does you might become fearful that the inventory you are undertaking is going to become unbearable. Do not concern yourself with the amount of work that is ahead of you. There will be time to do the writing. It is possible that your level of distress is increasing because of your growing awareness of the magnitude of the injuries you have endured and because the list of offenders appears greater than you had imagined it would be. You will get through this. Remember, if it is thorough you only have to do it this way once. Future inventories, should you choose to do them on an annual or semi-annual basis, will be easy and not likely to generate the apprehension you may have felt up to now.

Step-Sponsor Prompt

Inner Workings Profile

The following Exhibit is offered to give you a picture of the author's thoughts and actions connected with Tasks 5 and 6 for the Productive Entry addressing "Dad" in Exhibit 1.

Exhibit: 7
Title: Dad
Subtitle: Productive Entry

Thought Process

The author has completed the initial entry on his Dad (Exhibit 1). It addresses the injury he experienced with his Dad at the Boy Scout ceremony.

The author begins to reflect on the two questions in Task 5. When else have I felt this way? Who else has treated me this way? In reflecting on those questions, the author thinks to himself:

I know when I felt this way before! I felt humiliation and anger when my friend Bob was laughing at me when my father fell to the floor drunk. I felt humiliation when I was playing on a Little League team which my father coached and he used to call me names because I was fat and could not run very fast and my teammate Jimmy would laugh hysterically. I felt fear, anger, and powerlessness when this bully Jack used to take my lunch money in school. I felt this fear when I would lie in bed at night and hear a police siren in the street outside of our home and wondered whether or not it was headed for our house, and the anger would come many times when I expected that my Mom would stop my father from returning to our home after a breakup.

I have felt anger, impotence, powerlessness, and weakness many other times in my life. The situation at the Boy Scout ceremony is familiar too because I have frequently felt impotent when dealing with service departments in large companies like ABC Music Company.

Actions

The author examined the Master List to identify the people and institutions in the past and present with which he has felt similar emotions.

The author had previously identified Bob, Jim, and his Mom on his Master List. He now added Jack and the ABC Music Company to his list and generated additional Title Pages for them.

Step-Sponsor Prompt

Action

We are resuming here at Task 7. It will not be long before you will really understand the damage that you have had inflicted upon yourself. This understanding will help you to make sense out of the role that your most troublesome defects of character have played in your life because our defects of character develop to cope with the emotional discomfort we experience in events like the above Exhibits described. This insight will help you to define strategies for intervening on the problematic behaviors that you want to eliminate. We are getting ahead of ourselves and you are probably taking undue advantage of our rambling. We will leave you alone so you can get back to work.

~ Task 7 ~

Pull out the pages for each of the people or institutions that came to mind in Task 5. Identify and describe the wrong that each person or institution did to you one person or institution at a time, just as you did in Task 4.

You have put the page for the person you were first working on off to the side and brought to the forefront all the people or institutions that were brought to mind when you completed Task 7. You are going to work through the pile of Title Pages in front of you one at a time referring back to Task 4 if you need. It might also be helpful to review: the Productive Entry examples and the accompanying Inner Workings Profiles in Exhibits 1 through 4.

Step-Sponsor Prompt

Inner Workings Profile

The following Exhibit is offered to give you a picture of the author's thoughts and actions connected with Task 7 after completing the Productive Entry addressing Dad in Exhibit 1.

Exhibit: 8
Title: Dad
Subtitle: Productive Entry

Thought Process

This inventory will take me forever. It is easier just to leave the past where it was. (Nice try! Get back to work!)

Actions

The author pulled the following pages from the pile:

Mom because he has felt impotent and powerless over her unwillingness to get help for her husband's drinking problem.

Jim because he felt humiliated when Jim used to tease him about being fat.

Bob because Bob laughed and humiliated him.

Jack because he was a bully who used to take the author's lunch money from him.

ABC Music Company because he was unable to figure out how to cancel his membership and ended up getting charged for ten CD's that he could not return.

The author goes to work on writing out in detail each of the harms of others that were brought to mind when he thought about the questions in Task 5. In his description, he includes an approximation of when the wrong occurred, what the setting was, who the participants had been, and the feelings that had developed as well as the impact that the events have had on his life.

Step-Sponsor Prompt

Action

We are resuming here at Task 8. Keep up the faith. You are only three Tasks away from having completed Component 1.

~ Task 8 ~

When you complete each of the entries for the additional people or institutions, place their pages back in the unfinished pile.

Remember, you are working from a pile of individual sheets on the various people or institutions that you placed on your Master List of people or institutions that you have been harmed by. You had started with the first person or institution from your Master List and your reflections on the questions found in Component 1 - Task 5, which lead you to other people or institutions that have harmed you in a similar way. You have written about the wrongs that others have done toward you and are now returning to the person that you began with.

~ Task 9 ~

Pull the first person or institution that you began with back to the front of the pile and continue with the next wrong for that person or institution as you did in Task 4. Each time you add a new wrong for this person or institution, complete Tasks 5, 6, and 7.

Each time you describe another harm you endured, memories of other people, places, and events will start bubbling to the surface of your consciousness. As this is occurring pull the people or institutions from the pile so you can keep track of who you need to write about. This action of pulling the additional people or institutions from the pile as you are thinking about them will make it easier for you to stay on track with the main person or institution you are working on. You will begin to see that you are accumulating a good number of entries for the other people and institutions which will reduce the amount of work that you will need to do when you get to the point where you are working primarily on their Title Page.

Step-Sponsor Prompt

Inner Workings Profile

This Inner Workings Profile is offered to give you a picture of the author's thoughts and actions connected with Tasks 8 and 9.

Exhibit: 9
Title: Dad
Subtitle: Productive Entry

Thought Process

The author has completed Tasks 5, 6, and 7 following his initial entry on his Dad's Title Page. The author of the entry is beginning to understand how the guide is designed. He is filled with emotions and is perhaps a bit overwhelmed with the degree to which his feeling experiences are interconnected.

Actions

The author takes time out for a period of prayerful meditation.

The author has placed the other people and institutions back in the unfinished pile. He pulls Dad's Title Page back out and continues with the second wrong he associates with his Dad.

If there is not a second wrong for Dad, he moves on to the next person on his Master List.

The author continues working on completing each Task as appropriate.

Step-Sponsor Prompt

Think

The directions seem a little more complicated than the Tasks actually are. You will be moving back and forth between the current person or institution and the people or institutions you are reminded of. This approach is helpful for people who have difficulty remembering the chronology of the events in their lives and for the people with "memory holes" – virtually all of us! The work will begin to come quickly and you are likely to find that you have a difficult time writing as fast as you think. This is a very emotional process. You may be moved to tears. This is all right, though. The crying will slow you down and give your hand a rest.

Action

We are resuming here at Task 10 with the last Task in Component 1. Keep up the faith. You only have 15 more hours of writing. Sorry, that was not funny. We know it is hard, but if you do this completely you only have to dig this deep once and you will not have to put up with John's childish behavior again, I promise.

~ Task 10 ~

When you are finished moving back and forth between the various people and institutions, you are finished with Component 1.

Do not sit and dig for more material. All the information that God wants you to have for now is out. Call someone and talk if you are stuck. When you are unstuck, continue with Component 2. If you have written as much as comes to mind for each person or institution that you entered on your Master List for Component 1 then you are finished with this component. Clip the pile of pages together and place them in a folder or put them off to the side.

Step-Sponsor Prompts

Prayer

God, I am thankful to be finished with the painful examination of the injuries I have endured. I had feared that I would be weakened by the honest disclosure of the harms I have suffered. I was wrong. I do not feel weaker. I feel stronger. In my youth I was told not to "cry over spilled milk" and to leave the past in the past. I now understand that those directions were wrong. I have felt the pain that I once tried to dull with substances or addictive or controlling behaviors. I am more committed to recovery than ever before. Thank you.

Meditative Reflection

Picture yourself at the end of a scrapbook that has recorded all the harms you have ever experienced. The wrongs others had done to you are recorded in the pictures and mementos of that scrapbook. You have examined it honestly. The shame associated with the harmful behavior of others is beginning to fade. The scrapbook is private and can only be viewed by those to whom you have given permission. The scrapbook is yours to learn from. Feel free to share it with those who might benefit from the hope you are accumulating.

Mentorship

This might be a good time to make contact with your sponsor or another member of your support group to check in and let them know how you are doing. Do not get distracted with other issues. Keep your conversation on the road you have traveled thus far. Solicit the experience, strength, and hope of those who have traveled this road before you. If you can, spend a little time in the receipt of reflective support from a loving family member, it will help to normalize what you are experiencing at the moment. Choose a loved one you believe that you have a future with and the potential for healing the wounds you have identified. Do not share in great depth what you have been inventorying lest you leave them with a burden or prematurely open an amends process that you are not quite ready for.

If you are not able to make contact, then spend a moment writing about or reflecting on what you have to be grateful for regarding that loved one before continuing on with Component 2 where you will be analyzing your resentments.

Chapter 3: Component 2 - Analyze Our Resentments

In the previous chapter, you were guided through the first component of the inventory that focused on your past and present resentments. The writing may have been difficult at times, but your effort has already begun returning a reward in terms of the clarity of feeling that you now possess. Do not be discouraged by fatigue. You will be given the strength you need. The emotional drain that you are experiencing does not have to block your commitment to the work. Take breaks when you need them. Take a timed nap if you are too tired to continue but try to avoid getting involved in other distracting activities like work around the house, TV, or surfing the internet. The exhaustion is to be expected. You have completed a series of challenging and prospectively painful tasks.

You first created a list of all of the sources of personal harm in your life. In your detailed description of the individual wrongs, you began to identify the feelings and the impact that those harms have had on your life. You are now able to devote some energy to developing a better understanding of the resentments that grew from those injuries.

In this section we will present a series of Tasks in the form of questions that are intended to assist you in an analysis of your resentments. We hope that you will be inspired to identify patterns in the behaviors or personalities of those who have harmed you so you can better understand how to protect yourself from similar or continued harm in the future.

The thirteen Tasks that follow are offered as a method for organizing your thinking and guiding your analysis of your resentments. It is not necessary to answer any of the questions in writing but many people have found written notes helpful when attempting to share their insights with their sponsor or support group members. Members of your support system, your sponsor, and especially the recipient of your Fifth Step can use your reflections on the Task questions to better understand you. If you are working with a therapist the notes you take as you reflect on the questions raised during Component 2 can aid the two of you in the work you are doing to develop healthy boundaries and reasonable role expectations. If you choose not to prepare written responses to all of the questions, consider selecting those questions that focus on issues that you would like to explore further in your recovery.

The recovery text *Alcoholics Anonymous*[2] suggests that our resentments "could not be wished away" but they "... must be mastered" (1953, p. 37). The mastery, it would seem, could come if we could better understand those resentments and the story behind the people or institutions that we believed to have injured us. We encourage you to understand that the people who have harmed you were also sick (as you were) and that their hurtful behaviors are symptoms of their sickness. Let us examine the people and their behaviors so we can understand them as "sick" people. In Appendix C you will find a checklist to use as you work through this component.

Step-Sponsor Prompts

Prayer

God, my resentments have cost me nearly as much heartache and depression as the symptoms of my addictive illness and I want to be free of the darkness that has enshrouded me because of the ill will I hold toward others. I want to stop being at odds with anyone or anything.

Meditative Reflection

Picture the sheriff delivering an eviction notice to the people, events, and circumstances that have been living "rent free" in your head for the past few years or decades. You have allowed the harms done to you to play over and over again in your mind. Your recycling memories of the damages of the past have caused you to know greater hurt and depression, at times, than the original wrong caused. It is time for it to be done! Evict the squatters and reclaim your personal space.

～ Task 1 ～

How do these sick people act?

What are the behaviors that you find troubling or injurious? Do these behaviors appear to be normal or abnormal? Do the sick people in your life treat people, other than you, in a harmful manner? It might be helpful to examine all the people that have harmed you in the past to look for particular types of behaviors that you find hurtful. If you make a list of those behaviors you can work with your therapist or support group to develop strategies for the construction and maintenance of healthy boundaries for the present or future relationships you find stressful.

It may be difficult to distinguish normal from abnormal behaviors so consider getting input from those you trust as it may help you to discern between the two by getting input from someone you trust. If you notice that the people that hurt you have hurt others in ways that are similar to how you were hurt it may help you to better understand that you were not at fault for how people behaved toward you.

～ Task 2 ～

In what ways are the personalities of the wrongdoers similar?

It will be important for us to understand the behavioral patterns of the people who have injured us. It will help us in our efforts to teach people today how to treat us differently. We are commonly attracted to people with similar personalities. The people may dress differently or in some ways act very differently from others who had harmed us. If we expect to attract different people, we must first understand what we have been attracted to in the people from our past. Additionally, if we do not develop our understanding of the similarities, we will end up getting hurt repeatedly, remain resentful, and feel hopeless.

～ Task 3 ～

Are there patterns to the way that I have responded to their sick behavior?

We are quick to say that it is always the other person, but the common denominator in all those hurtful relationships was ourselves. Do not misunderstand this question to mean that you are to blame for how others have hurt you. The question is designed to help you begin to identify the parts of you that draw you into a relationship with people that are going to hurt you. An examination of the ways that you consistently behave in problem relationships will reveal a great deal to you about your own defects of character. The identification of these patterns will serve as the foundation for your journey through Steps 6 and 7. These crucial steps in the recovery process usually get very little attention.

～ Task 4 ～

What did I hope to get from these people or institutions that they were apparently not ready or able to provide?

Identify what your expectations of these people or institutions might have been. If you are unclear about your expectations, you might examine the physical, emotional, social, spiritual, and financial disappointments you might have experienced with the institution or person in question. Once you have identified what you were looking for from these hurtful relationships you are likely to pinpoint needs that routinely go unmet for you. Take your discoveries to therapy and or to your support group relationships for help with ideas for getting these important needs met in ways that are both healthy and mutually rewarding. Additionally, it might help you to explore the stories behind why certain people were not ready or seemingly unable to provide what you needed.

~ Task 5 ~

What is the nature of my relationship with these people today?

Oftentimes we continue to tolerate mistreatment from the people who have caused us great harm in the past. We make no effort to redefine the relationship and establish our needs and limits; so we repeat the past. Examine what you have done about the relationships that have caused you pain and what, if anything, you need to change. This work will continue in greater depth when you begin to examine your defects of character in Step 6, but it is wise to get a sense of what you are seeking now.

~ Task 6 ~

Do I find myself getting disappointed frequently?

When you review the relationships of your past in an effort to analyze your resentments make sure to examine the pattern of your disappointment with people, institutions, or society as a whole. Have you come to believe that it is not possible to have a mutually rewarding relationship? Have you given up hope of finding people on whom you can rely? If so, trust the success of those who have journeyed before you and look for ways of being of service to those who appear less fortunate than you. It will renew your faith. It may be very important to share your reflections on these questions with your therapist or sponsor because you may find yourself reacting to people in the present because of past disappointments you have endured.

~ Task 7 ~

Do my relationships appear a bit lopsided?

Relationships in which you give more than you are receiving can be hurtful even when the other person has not intended to hurt you in any way. Mutual relationships are difficult to maintain because they require a great deal of honesty and openness. Relationships can easily become lopsided when the partners have not learned how to keep God in the center of the relationship. Painfully lopsided relationships can be changed into mutually rewarding ones in which both partners give and receive. The key obstacle to the reformation is unwillingness on the part of either partner to examine himself or herself and the ways in which his or her defects of character are negatively affecting the relationship. It might be helpful for you to examine the ways or times in which your current relationships appear to be lopsided and discuss your insights with your therapist or support group members.

~ Task 8 ~

Do I have people in my life today, who are like hurtful people from my past, who I currently allow to get too close to me?

For example, if you struggled with bullies in the past in relationships that were harmful to you, there is a good chance that you have bullies in your life today. If you are going to be freed from the resentments toward past bullies and come to understand them as troubled spirits, you will need to examine your present relationships closely. The hurt you suffer in your relationships with the bullies of today will fuel the resentments of the past. It may seem as if we are young children incapable of protecting ourselves from the monsters of our past. Generally, that means that there are some monsters in your present life with which you must contend.

Alcoholics Anonymous[2] (1953) encourages us to look for ways to show these sick people the same "tolerance, pity, and patience that we would cheerfully grant a sick friend" (p. 41). What an order! The prospect of being of service to these people is likely to be the furthest thought from your mind right now, but that is the direction you will need to head. It might be easier to find ways of being of service if you look even further into their lives. The notes you make for yourself on this question could be of great value to you when you are working on your Sixth and Eighth Steps.

~ Task 9 ~

Who are these sick people and what do I know about their lives?

What do you know about the injuries they have endured? We know very little about why humans hurt other humans, but we know for certain that hurt people hurt other people. Developing a clearer understanding of the purpose of someone's behavior can be of enormous value in understanding the wrong they have committed and placing it into a sharper perspective. That is not to say that we support the habit of making excuses for other people's mistreatment of us. The relief you would gain from such a strategy would be fleeting. We are not asking you to create justifications for someone else's hurtful behavior. The challenge here is to understand that, in some cases, the wrongdoer was living life according to a pattern or a reaction that had nothing to do with you. You, through perhaps no fault of your own, were in the wrong place at the wrong time. Consider this example:

Harry is walking through a patient wing of the local hospital to visit an elderly relative who is recovering from a recent fall. As he passes an open doorway to a patient room, he notices Bob, a newcomer to his home group, lying in bed staring out the window. He decides to be friendly as he has come to think highly of Bob's commitment to recovery and pays him a quick visit. Harry enters the room to see if he could be of service and is greeted with an angry outburst from Bob who screams obscenities and chastises Harry for entering where he is not welcome. Harry leaves quickly to avoid further attacks and wanders down the hallway somewhat dazed by the rude and ungrateful reception he has received from Bob. Along the way to his relative's room, Harry runs into Sam, another member of his home group, and proceeds to assassinate Bob's character for how Bob has treated him. Harry is good and mad and certain that his anger is justified. He would never speak to Bob again and regrets ever deciding to try to be of service. Sam knows better than to interrupt Harry in his revengeful counterattack on Bob because Harry believes himself to be the victim of a personal attack. When Harry exhausts the emotional fuel he is burning, Sam suggests that Harry might have it all wrong. He explains that Bob and his family had been in a car accident that morning and that Bob was the only survivor. The anger quickly drains out of Harry's face as he listens to the tragic account of the accident. Bob has not launched a personal attack on Harry. Bob had just launched an attack and Harry was available.

Many times we can become obsessed with the resentment associated with the wrongs we have had to endure. We have often wrongly assumed that there must be something inherently wrong with us or people would not have treated us so poorly. Often the harms others had caused us had little or nothing to do with who we were or how we behaved. Others were troubled and we became their victims. This is an important point to reflect upon because many of us have spent years believing we were flawed because of the way that others had treated us. Injury can surely cause flaws, but we were not injured because we were flawed. We had decided that our brokenness had somehow caused others to disregard or neglect our needs or to behave abusively. We have come to understand through a similar analysis of our resentments that our perceptions were flawed, not our personhood.

~ Task 10 ~

What do you know about the way the people who harmed you felt or feel about the wrongs that they committed toward you?

Many times we harbor resentments for the wrongdoers in our lives because we assume that we were the only ones injured by their behaviors. It is odd to consider a perpetrator as a victim, but we have found the strategy helpful when trying to rid ourselves of deep-seated resentments that fester and continually diminish our spiritual well-being. The fact that the wrongdoer was also hurt in the behavior that injured us is not a far-fetched idea. Think about the guilt, shame, and remorse that drove you into recovery or that appeared once you had decided to get help and took the time to look around at the wreckage. If the hurt you felt about the wrong you had done others was real, then it is possible that the wrongdoers in your life may also have been injured by the way that they have treated you. It might be helpful for you to imagine what the inventories of those who have harmed you would look like.

~ Task 11 ~

Can you acquire the humility needed for compassion?

In Component 3 you will have an opportunity for a closer examination of this principle. Your reflection on the wrongs you have committed toward others, perhaps many years in the past, is likely to generate a great deal of discomfort in you. You will gain understanding into the nature of the people that have harmed you as you explore your own patterns of wrongs at greater depth. Consider the ways in which the perpetrators on your resentment list may have injured themselves by their neglect or mistreatment of you. You may be able to transform your anger and bitterness into compassion. We have found that, many times, the people we loved to resent were a great deal more like us than they were different. Those painful insights one day lead us to emotional freedom and a spiritual awakening, but the journey begins with a large piece of humble pie as we identify the similarities between the personality traits of those who have hurt us and our own traits.

~ Task 12 ~

Examine how the resentment has injured you.

You can use resentment to continue drinking, obsessing, acting out sexually, overeating, gambling, etc., etc. The list is endless because there is an endless number of ways to hurt ourselves and to injure others. A quick written inventory of the ways in which the resentment (not the wrong or wrongdoer) has injured you will allow you to understand more about your self injurious behaviors. If you are not planning to include yourself on the Master List for Component 3, then this is a good place to do some soul searching that you can share with others you rely on for support in your recovery.

~ Task 13 ~

Do your resentments serve a function in your life that you fear you cannot live without?

Resentments maintain a level of emotional and spiritual negativity that can provide nourishment (however empty of spiritual calories it is) for us if we are starved for intimacy and we are willing to accept the drama of a smoldering resentment in place of a life with true purpose. Our pain can become an important force in our life. It is easy to fall into the trap of believing that we are our pain and suffering. The person who clings to the pain, resentment, and shame will know only suffering. Life will be little more than an endurance contest. Resentment is often very passionate, emotionally exhilarating, and a source of potential attention from others. Many newcomers to the 12 Step recovery process will suffer under the idea that they are their illness. They will wear their illness like a shield, using it to explain away their own unwanted or unacceptable behavior. They will blame their illness for blocking their road to happiness and peace. The disease and the person will be seen as one and the same. However, we are not our illness. We have an illness that a 12 Step recovery program can arrest and help to promote lasting health. Having an addiction or co-addiction is not a death sentence for the body, mind, or spirit unless we order it to be so.

Keep the notes you make for yourself on this question because you will be able to use the insights you gain here to address the character defects in your Sixth and Seventh Steps.

Step-Sponsor Prompts

Prayer

God, you know better than I the pain I have endured. You know that my use of addictive substances or behaviors never addressed the problem. I no longer want to deaden the pain or the joy of living. Show me ways to learn from all that I have experienced.

Meditative Reflection

Picture yourself with a new tool kit for understanding and responding to life. The kit has many new tools that you are still quite unfamiliar with. You can learn how to use the tools to understand the behaviors of your fellows better and to help you stay out of harm's way. You once had only the tool of blame in your kit. You would blame either other people or yourself for the poor quality of your life, but you never got beyond blaming. The questions you have just reflected on have given you many new tools for change. There is much for which to be grateful.

Chapter 4: Component 3 - List Our Wrongs

In Component 2 - Analyze Our Resentments you had an opportunity to develop your understanding of the recurring thoughts and feelings that create moods of resentment. Identifying and understanding your resentments is the first step toward their removal in the Fifth, Seventh, and Ninth Steps. The freedom you seek from the oppressive power of resentment is within your reach. You must first clean your side of the street through a thorough examination of your wrongs.

This Component will redirect you back through the same pages of your life that you inventoried in Component 1. This time, however, you will examine the people and institutions you have wronged. Some of them may have appeared on the Master List in Component 1 because of the harm that they caused you but this part of the inventory is not about the way that you were hurt by those people or institutions. This Component is about how you have hurt them or others who will be appearing in your inventory work for the first time. The Tasks marked 1 through 10 are very similar to those developed in Component 1, but you will look at them through the eyes of the wrongdoer, not the victim.

Remember, this is not a term paper. You will not be penalized if you jump from one time period to another. The important thing is that you allow your feeling memories to guide you. In addition, remember thoroughness is the key to success.

Step-Sponsor Prompts

This might be a good time to engage in a moment of prayer or meditative reflection. This component is likely to dredge up a good deal of emotional muck. Keep in mind that these wrongs are in the past and you never have to repeat these behaviors again.

Prayer

God, I am grateful for the insights that I have gained from the examination of my injuries. The tools for understanding the troubling behavior of others are still new to me, but I can see the reward that will come from the freedom from resentment that awaits me. Give me the courage I need now to examine the wrongs others have suffered because of the flaws in my character.

Meditative Reflection

Picture yourself restocking your ship for a return voyage to your homeport. You are preparing to come back to the place where real and lasting change can be made. This part of the journey might seem more frightening because you will be looking at the damage you have inflicted. Do not let the fear stop you. You cannot change those who have hurt you, but you can change those parts of yourself that have caused you to inflict pain on others. Component 3 is the beginning of that process. Peaceful sailing!

Stop

Read the entire chapter before you begin writing. Read and complete numbered sections before moving on to the next Task. Complete all of the items, Tasks 1 through 10, before beginning Component 4. Some of the Tasks will appear to be unnecessary, but they are important because they are designed to cause you to stop and reflect on your work.

Before you begin your written work on the Tasks for Component 3 below, let us review all 10 of the Tasks. The guide uses ten specific and measureable tasks that guide you through the process of completing Component 3 of your Fourth Step. They are listed here as an introduction for future reference.

1. Create a Master List of every person or institution that you have ever wronged.

2. Create a separate Title Page for each person or institution you have identified on the Master List and place the name of each person or institution on the top of his or her own Title Page.

3. Place the stack of Title Pages in front of you and choose which person or institution to begin with.

4. On the Title Page, for the person or institution you have chosen, describe in detail one of the wrongs that you have done to that person or institution.

5. The guide is designed to use your feeling memories to identify other similar life experiences. Your reflections on the following two questions will remind you of the other people or institutions which have harmed you.

    When have I felt this way?

    Who else has treated me this way?

6. Look at your Master List and identify the people or institutions that you have harmed in a similar fashion. If your reflections on the two questions in Task 5 brought new people or institutions to mind, add them to the Master List and give them their own Title Page.

7. Pull out the pages for each of the people or institutions that came to mind in Task 5, identify and describe the wrong that you did to each person or institution just as you did in Task 4.

8. When you complete each of the entries for the additional people or institutions, place their pages back in the unfinished pile.

9. Pull the first page back out and continue with the next wrong for that person or institution as you did in Task 4. Each time you add a new wrong for this person or institution, complete Tasks 5, 6, and 7.

10. When you are finished moving back and forth between the various people and institutions, you are finished with Component 3.

~ Task 1 ~

Create a Master List of every person or institution that you have ever wronged.

You will want to keep your Master List handy because you will probably add people or institutions to it as you complete the 10 numbered Tasks for this Component. When you are developing your list, do not exclude people merely because they have also hurt you or because you believe that you were only getting even or reacting appropriately to the harms they caused you. If you discover additional harms make note of the memories so you can return to Component 1 to add these or other amendments before continuing in your inventory. Do not concern yourself with keeping the list of the victims in chronological order or with ordering them in terms of the degree of hurt you have inflicted. Neither formula for ordering the list is required. Simply list the people or institutions that have caused harm as they occur to you.

Avoid the tendency to exclude someone from your list because you do not believe that listing them is fair. Here is a collection of some INVALID reasons for excluding someone or some institution from the master list for Component 3 - Task 1:

- You did not mean to hurt them
- The person has caused you or others injury
- You did not know any better
- The person or institution was harmed accidentally by the behavior you intended for others
- The person or institution is not aware of the wrong
- I don't need to address him or her because I have already been forgiven by them
- You were doing what you were taught by others
- You have been hurt by many people so it does not matter

There are many other seemingly legitimate reasons for excluding someone from the list but there is no excusing hurtful behavior. The harms you caused were real if it felt real regardless of whatever else you know about the person, the circumstances, or possible motivations.

~ Task 2 ~

Create a separate Title Page for each person or institution you have identified on the Master List and place the name of each person or institution on the top of his or her own Title Page.

You will probably need numerous sheets so have a supply handy. It might be easier to keep track of your work if you use loose-leaf sheets of paper because there are bound to be corrections that will become messy if you try to use a bound notebook whose pages are not easily detachable. Clip a few blank sheets to the Title Page for each person so you do not have to stop the flow of your writing to find extra paper when you are working. You will end up with quite a few individual pages, so you might want to number the pages belonging to each person or institution on the Master List so you do not lose track and keep them in a folder marked Component 3 - List Our Wrongs.

You will prepare a Title Page for each person on your list even if you do not yet know what it is that you want to write about. If the person or institution comes to mind as being wronged by you then create a Title Page.   Your entries will be numbered for each person and you will begin your written work on the Title Page for that person or institution. Before you continue on to Component 3 - Task 3 double check your Master List to be sure that you have a Title Page for each person.

~ Task 3 ~

Place the stack of Title Pages in front of you and choose which person or institution you will work with first.

It does not matter which person or institution you begin with because you will refer continually to these Title Pages as you move back and forth between all the people and institutions on the Master List. You can pick the person that you are currently the closest to or select a person for whom your wrongs were minimal.

Step-Sponsor Prompts

Think

Task 4 will direct you to begin writing a detailed description of the wrongs you committed. Before moving to that task, let us first review samples of Productive and Unproductive Entries for Task 4. Following each entry, you will read a Step-Sponsor Prompt - Inner Workings Profile.

Snapshot

Exhibit 10 is an example of a Productive Entry that clearly focuses the responsibility for the wrong on the author and examines the ways in which the victim was harmed.

Exhibit: 10
Title: Boy Scout Troop # 128
Subtitle: Productive Entry

When I was ten years old, I got together with some of my neighborhood friends and broke into the church basement to trash the new gear the Boy Scout troop had just purchased. I was a member of that troop and we had worked for nearly two years to raise the money for the new tents and other pieces of equipment. My friends and I broke the lock on the door, cut the tents to shreds, and smashed the cook stoves, lanterns, and other breakable equipment.

The troop had worked hard to raise the $2,000 for the new equipment and we had been so proud. I was all jazzed with excitement when we were breaking into the basement. It felt dangerous and righteous at the same time. I remember thinking this was crazy, but who cares!

In the weeks that followed, the local paper ran several articles on the event and the "warped thinking" that went into such a "senseless" destruction of property. When I heard of the articles, the feelings of exhilaration and revenge I had felt were replaced by shame and self-loathing. I could never again face the guys from the troop and I spent a lot of time avoiding the guys who were involved with me that night. It was one of the worst summers of my life.

To this day I avoid discussions that involve scouting and feel sick when I see a young boy in a scouting uniform. I remember how proud I was to get mine and how fearful of it I had become when it hung in my closet for all those years. The troop never deserved my punishment.

Step-Sponsor Prompt

Inner Workings Profile

Exhibit 11 is offered to give you a picture of the author's thoughts and actions connected with the Task for the Productive Entry addressing Boy Scout Troop # 128 in Exhibit 10.

Exhibit: 11
Title: Boy Scout Troop # 128
Subtitle: Productive Entry

Thought Process

The author reflects back on the times in his life when his actions caused other people or institutions harm:

His thoughts go immediately to his memory of the injury he endured by his Dad at the Boy Scout ceremony. However, this time he would examine the events from a different viewpoint. Now he is looking only at the way he dealt with his feelings of injury through the use of revenge.

Actions

The author describes the setting:

Ten years old at his neighborhood church which was the headquarters of his former Boy Scout Troop # 128

He describes the specific details associated with the wrong:

He was responsible for breaking into the church and destroying most of the troop's equipment.

He identifies the key people present at the time of his injury:

The troop members, who were the real victims, and his fellow vandals.

He identifies and underlines the feelings that he and the others were experiencing.

His feelings were: jazzed, excited, dangerous, righteous, exhilaration, vengeful, shame, self-loathing, and fear.

He describes the impact the event had on him at the time and since then:

At first the feelings of exhilaration and revenge left him feeling pleased that others had now felt the pain that he felt the night his father fell on the floor at the Boy Scouts ceremony. The feelings associated with "getting even" were replaced by shame and self-loathing when the real impact of his emotional violence had been felt. Since the event he has held deep resentment for himself for having struck out in anger at innocent victims.

Step-Sponsor Prompt

Snapshot

Exhibit 12 is an example of an Unproductive Entry. It is offered to help you avoid the common pitfalls associated with Unproductive Entries. It is intended to show how <u>not</u> to describe a wrong. The elements that are considered unproductive will be in bold.

Notes to Myself:

Exhibit: 12
Title: Boy Scout Troop # 128
Subtitle: Unproductive Entry

My Dad ruined my life when I was ten years old. Heck, he had ruined it years before, but what he did at the Boy Scout Troop ceremony was one of the worst events of my life and I will never forgive him for it. He showed up drunk and made such a scene that I was forced to leave without getting my merit badges. My Mom and I left in tears as several of the parents whispered and some of my troop members giggled. **I was full of <u>anger</u> and <u>rage</u> that night and vowed to get even with them all. Who could blame me for wanting <u>revenge</u>? Someone needed to teach them a lesson.**

Two of my closest friends and I broke into the church basement to trash the new gear the troop had recently purchased. When I was a member of that troop, I had worked for nearly two years to raise the money for the new tents and other pieces of equipment. My friends and I broke the lock on the door, cut the tents to shreds, and smashed the cook stoves, lanterns, and other breakable equipment. I was all <u>jazzed</u> with <u>excitement</u> when we were breaking into the basement. It felt <u>dangerous</u> and <u>righteous</u> at the same time. I remember thinking this was crazy, but who cares! **No one would ever find out who did it.**

In the weeks that followed, the local paper ran several articles on the event and the "warped thinking" that went into such a "senseless" destruction of property. When I heard of the articles, the feelings of <u>exhilaration</u> and <u>revenge</u> I had felt were replaced by <u>shame</u> and <u>self-loathing</u>. I could never again face my fellow troop members and I spent a lot of time avoiding the guys who were involved with me that night. It was one of the worst summers of my life.

Maybe the people who thought my Dad was funny would see the humor in their wrecked gear. They would not make fun of me again. My father never once said he was sorry for what he did to me that night and how he ruined the summer for me. The scout troop would replace the equipment, but I would never be able to face the troop again. Dad had seen to that.

To this day, I avoid discussions that involve scouting and feel <u>sick</u> when I see a young boy in a scouting uniform. I remember how proud I was to get mine and how <u>fearful</u> of it I had become when it hung in my closet for all those years. **The troop never deserved my punishment, but I did not deserve the <u>humiliation</u> either.** I vowed never to do that to my kids.

Step-Sponsor Prompt

Inner Workings Profile

Exhibit 13 is offered to give you a picture of the author's thoughts and actions connected with Task 4 for the Unproductive Entry addressing Boy Scout Troop # 128 in Exhibit 12.

Exhibit: 13
Title: Boy Scout Troop # 128
Subtitle: Unproductive Entry

Thought Process

The author reflects back on the times in his life when he has wronged others:

He identifies the time he destroyed the Boy Scout troop gear. He feels ashamed of his behavior, but imagines that anyone in his place would have done the same thing. He is in a real conflict. He knows that he was wrong, but he cannot keep focused on his wrongs because he is preoccupied with the injuries he suffered and believes that others were more to blame than he was.

Actions

The author describes the setting:

Ten years old in his neighborhood church which was the headquarters of his former Boy Scout Troop # 128.

He describes the specific details associated with the wrong:

He was responsible for breaking into the church and destroying most of the troop's equipment but rationalizes that he is getting even with those who hurt him first.

He identifies the key people present at the time of his injury:

The troop members (who were the real victims) and the other boys he hung with who were involved in the vandalism. He wrongly includes himself as a victim of the shame and humiliation that his father caused him; he focuses the blame for his behavior on his father.

He identifies and underlines the feelings that he and others were experiencing:

His feelings were: anger, rage, revenge, jazzed, excited, dangerous, righteous, exhilaration, vengeful, shame, self-loathing, sick, fearful, and humiliation.

He makes excuses for his behavior:

His fellow troop members laughed at his Dad, and he was justified in destroying their gear. He claims that his Dad was responsible for the worst summer of his life because he holds his Dad, rather than himself, responsible for the destruction of the troop's gear and the shame that followed.

He describes the impact the event had on him at the time and since then:

He attempts to describe the impact that the shame had on him, but he does not take any responsibility for his own behavior. So he will not be relieved of the hurt when he shares it in his Fifth Step.

Step-Sponsor Prompts

Think

The example above correctly addresses all the facts associated with the wrong that occurred, but the focus here is on the wrongs of the boy's father and his fellow troop members and not on the wrongs of the boy. It was painful for the adult author to examine his behavior in the light of his older wisdom. He was truly ashamed of himself, but the blame was placed on the person he believed was the cause of the wrong – his father. The author of this example is not likely to feel much in the way of relief and the amends he will make in the Ninth Step is likely to be shallow at best if, in fact, he sees the need to make amends at all! Let us take a moment to review what you have done so far before you begin writing about the wrongs you have committed.

- Created a Master List of all the people and institutions that you have harmed in Task 1.
- Created a separate Title Page for each person or institution you identified on the Master List and placed the name of each person or institution on the top of their own page in Task 2.
- Placed the stack of Title Pages in front of you and chose which person or institution to begin with in Task 3.
- Read through the description of Task 4.
- Examined the Snapshot example of a Productive Entry in Exhibit 10 to view an sample of how a Productive Entry of your wrong might be developed.
- Examined the Inner Workings Profile in Exhibit 11 to develop insight into the thoughts and actions of the author when he created the Productive Entry.
- Examined the Snapshot example of an Unproductive Entry in Exhibit 12.
- Examined the Inner Workings Profile in Exhibit 13 to develop insight into the thoughts and actions of the author when he created the Unproductive Entry.

Action

We will now continue with Task 4.

~ Task 4 ~

On the Title Page for the person or institution that you have chosen, describe in detail one of the wrongs that you have done to that person or institution

In your description, include an approximation of when the wrong occurred, what the setting was, who the participants had been, and exactly what the wrong was that you committed. Each time you complete a description of a wrong in Task 4, try to describe the feelings, both past and present that are associated with the wrong. The following two questions might be helpful for you to consider once you have described the facts.

How did the wrong make me feel at the time?

Describe your feeling reaction in as much detail as you are capable of. If you are having difficulty naming the feeling, you can choose "comfortable" or "uncomfortable" or see Appendix F for a list of feeling words.

How has the wrong affected my life since?

This question is asking that you look at the ways that you believe both you and the victims have suffered from the harm since then. You may have already made what you believe is a satisfactory amends to the person or institution that you harmed. That is great! It is still important to include them in your inventory. The effort you put into these descriptions will be of enormous value to you when you begin to examine what your defects of character are doing for you and why it is so difficult to give them up. It does not matter whether or not the person or institution is aware of your wrong; you need to write about it anyway.

As you are describing the wrongs that you committed against persons or institutions, avoid making excuses for your behavior as you saw the author do in the Unproductive Entry in Exhibit 12. It is especially important that you do not include the harm they may have done to you. A clear understanding of your wrongs will be essential to the construction of the arch to freedom that you are building. If you excuse your wrongs by pointing out the faults of others, you may not experience the relief from this soul-searching inventory that you desire and deserve. For example, it is not productive to write: "I, like most people, have been dishonest on my income tax returns." You can discuss your resentments for the IRS in Component 1. This part is not about resentments. It is focused on your wrongs. For right now, stick to how you were wrong. The success of the work you will undertake in your Sixth and Seventh Steps will largely depend on your honesty and singular focus here.

Step-Sponsor Prompt

Think

Before you move onto the next harm that you have caused a person or institution, complete Tasks 5 and 6. Theses Tasks will not require that you write anything. You will only need an open mind and heart. Let your feelings be your guide. You will come back to the original person when you are finished identifying other people or institutions you have harmed in similar ways.

~ Task 5 ~

The guide is designed to use your feeling memories to identify other similar life experiences. Your reflections on the following two questions will remind you of the other people or institutions whom you have harmed. Consider the following questions:

When else have I felt this way?
What other people or institutions have I treated this way?

This is important because oftentimes the shame we feel from the harm that we have caused one person triggers our feeling memory of all the other hurts we have committed. The opening of the floodgate can cause considerable depression if we are not diligently working through the Twelve Steps. Clearing away the wreckage of the past is vitally important to the development of a spiritual life that will ensure continued recovery.

Step-Sponsor Prompt

Think

Relapse will occur for a variety of reasons, but commonly guilt and shame related to the wreckage of our past can create a slippery slope upon which many of our fellows have lost their footing. Draw hope from the knowledge that your efforts to move through Steps 4 through 6 will give you many opportunities to address and resolve guilt and shame as well as other potential relapse triggers. Time to get back to work.

~ Task 6 ~

After reflecting on the questions in Task 5 look at your Master List and identify the people or institutions that you have harmed in a similar fashion. If your reflections on these two questions above brought new people or institutions to mind, add them to the Master List and give them their own Title Page.

The size of your Master List is likely to grow as it did in Component 1 but that is not reason for concern. Your work is no longer about a contest to be endured but an act of loving and honest examination of the damage you have caused and much of that can be repaired. There is far more that you can do about the harms you have caused than you can about the hurts you have endured. You are now more than halfway through your Fourth Step and you are not likely to have to search as deep and long to find your wrongs as you did to unearth your injuries.

The critical self-analysis you are conducting will pay you handsomely for your investment of time and honesty. Imagine that there is going to come a time when you no longer have to look in the rearview mirror of your life with regret. You will get through this. The first time is the toughest and if it is thorough you only have to do it at this depth once. Future inventories, should you choose to do them on an annual or semi-annual basis will be easy and not likely to generate the apprehension you have felt up to now. Do not focus on the size of your Master List.

Step-Sponsor Prompt

Inner Workings Profile

Exhibit 14 will give you a picture of the author's thoughts and actions connected with Tasks 5 and 6 for the Productive Entry addressing Boy Scout Troop # 128.

Exhibit: 14
Title: Boy Scoot Troop # 128
Subtitle: Productive Entry

Thought Process

The author has completed the entry (Exhibit 10) that addresses the injury he has caused others in connection with his destruction of the property of the Boy Scout troop. He examined the feelings that he had at the time of the incident and the ways in which he believes that the incident has affected his life.

He identified anger, rage, shame, jazzed, danger, and righteousness as the key feelings from the incident.

The author reflects on the questions in Task 5. When else have I felt this way? What other people or institutions have I treated this way? In reflecting on the above questions, the author thinks to himself:

I know when I felt this way before! I felt this ashamed and angry at myself when I was in the third grade and I hit Joey when he said I was fat, and when I was in high school and got turned down by Nancy for the prom and broke the windshield of her car with a rock, and when I was passed over and did not get the promotion I desired when I worked at What's-A-Matter-With-You Treatment Facility and I gossiped about Mary and tried to get her fired.

Actions

The author examined the Master List to identify the people and institutions in the past and present with which he has felt similar emotions.

The author takes out the pages with Joey and Nancy's names on them, as well as the page that belongs to What's-A-With-Matter-You Treatment Facility.

The author realized that he forgot all about Mary and adds her to the Master List and creates a Title Page for her.

Step-Sponsor Prompt

Action

Time to resume work on your inventory with Task 7.

~ Task 7 ~

Pull out the pages for each of the people or institutions that come to mind and identify and describe the wrongs that you committed against each person or institution on your list just as you did in Task 4.

You have put the page for the person you were first working on to the side and brought to the forefront all the people or institutions that were brought to mind when you completed Task 5. You are going to work through the pile of Title Pages in front of you one at a time referring back to Task 4 if you need.

Step-Sponsor Prompt

Inner Workings Profile

Exhibit 15 creates a picture of the author's thoughts and actions connected with Task 7 for the Productive Entry addressing Boy Scout Troop # 128 (Exhibit 10).

Exhibit: 15
Title: Boy Scout Troop # 128
Subtitle: Productive Entry

Thought Process

I am not sure that it was such a good idea to begin this guide, but I am more than halfway done and I am going to finish this. I cannot wait until I can give this inventory guide to the people I sponsor so I can get them to work this hard.

Actions

After he gathers all the pages, he goes to work on writing out in detail each of the wrongs that his feeling memories brought to mind when he thought about the questions in Task 5.

In writing his description, he includes an approximation of when the wrong occurred, what the setting was, who the participants had been, and exactly what the wrong was that he had done. After writing the facts, he explains how he felt about his behavior at the time and what impact it has had on his life in order to complete Task 4.

When he is finished, he returns to the sheet he began with on Boy Scout Troop # 128. If he has other wrongs to describe, he does so in detail. If not, he continues with the next person or institution on his Master List of wrongs.

Step-Sponsor Prompt

Action

It is time to resume work on your inventory with Task 8.

~ Task 8 ~

When you complete each of the entries for the additional people or institutions, place their pages back in the unfinished pile.

Step-Sponsor Prompt

Think

Remember, you are working from a pile of individual sheets on the various people or institutions that you placed on your Master List of people and institutions that you have harmed. You had started with the first person or institution from your Master List and your reflections on the questions found at Component 3 - Task 5, which led you to other people or institutions that you have harmed in a similar way. You have written about your wrongs toward the others you identified and you are returning to the person that you began with.

~ Task 9 ~

Pull the first page back out and continue with the next wrong for that person as you did in Task 1. Each time you add a new wrong for this initial person or institution, complete Tasks 5, 6, and 7.

As we noted in Component 1, the directions seem a little more complicated than the Tasks actually are. You will be moving back and forth between the current person or institution and the people or institutions you are reminded of. You will find it easy to remember people, places, and events because you will be using feeling triggers to remind you, and feelings never forget a face!

The words will come quickly and you are likely to find that you have a difficult time writing as fast as you can think.

~ Task 10 ~

When you are finished moving back and forth between the various people and institutions, you are finished with Component 3.

Do not sit and dig for more material. All the information that God wants you to have for now is out. Call someone and talk if you are stuck. When you are unstuck, continue with Component 4.

Step-Sponsor Prompts

You have demonstrated a strong commitment to recovery and the majority of the housecleaning is complete. This might be a good time to engage in a moment of prayer or meditative reflection. Take a moment to ground yourself with prayer and meditation. The prayer or method of reflection you choose is up to you.

Prayer

God, thank you for providing me with the courage and strength to complete the journey through my past. Help me not to run before I have the opportunity to experience all that is promised me in the new life of recovery. Be with me when I go forward to share these discoveries with my sponsor or advisor in the Fifth Step.

Meditative Reflection

Imagine lying back in your raft as you emerge from the last stretch of turbulent water. Your journey deposits you in a large pool of water whose bottom is clearly visible. There is still some work to be done before you can rest comfortably. The journey has been long and difficult at times but the memory of the trip will last a lifetime and serve as an inspiration to those you are chosen to guide in the future.

Chapter 5: Component 4 - Straighten out the Past if We Can

In the last chapter, you completed Component 3. The Tasks provided you with an opportunity to fully examine the ways in which you have harmed other people and institutions. The work was tiring and emotionally draining, but all the secrets are now on paper where they belong. In your Fifth Step you can share them (along with your resentments) by reading all that you wrote in Components 1 and 3. It might also be helpful to share with your sponsor, therapist, or advisor what you learned about yourself in Component 2 that represented the analysis of your resentments. You have arrived at the final component. You will need to shift your focus from the past to the future to explore your motivation for restoring the ruins of the past.

Many of us begin our inventory with a focus on our desire to clear away the wreckage of the past. In many cases, our willingness to address the brokenness of interpersonal relationships is strong because we are able to see that the people who we care for have been hurt. In some cases, we have attempted to maintain our relationships with these people especially in the cases involving family members and long-time friends. We have limped along in these relationships during recovery with the idea that we would straighten out what had gone wrong if we could.

If we are sincere about our desire to practice the principles of recovery in all of our affairs, this Fourth Component of the personal inventory is the beginning of the amends process that will be further developed in Steps 8 and 9. Examine what you have done about the relationships that have caused you pain and what, if anything, you need to change. This work will continue in greater depth when you embark on the examination of your defects of character. It is wise to get a sense of what you are looking for now.

The first three components of the guide have focused your attention on the past. You have identified the sources of pain in your life and are in the process of developing a better understanding of your character defects. This Fourth Component is not intended to push you into the recovery tasks associated with making amends. The purpose is to help you identify which relationships you would like to rebuild through the practice of Steps 6, 7, 8, and 9. The Tasks are presented as reflective questions that may help you to focus your dreams and plans for the future. They are not intended to produce more writing. In fact, the Tasks do not require a written response. If you decide to write out responses to the questions, that is fine. You can use them for future reference when you get to your Sixth Step.

~ Task 1 ~

Which relationships from your combined two Master Lists (developed in Components 1 and 3) would you like to improve?

Make a list of the relationships you would like to improve for future reference when working with your sponsor, therapist, or support group members. Do not concern yourself with whether or not the other person might be interested. The focus here is on what you desire for the future. Remember that we have the power, if we remain sober, to change the way we relate to others. Do not be surprised if people that had come to remain quite separate from you begin to demonstrate their attraction to the change that they see in you.

~ Task 2 ~

What personal character changes will you need to explore in order to make a positive contribution to your relationship with these people?

If some of those changes are apparent to you now, make a list for future reference when you get to work on your Sixth Step.

~ Task 3 ~

Which relationships do you view as being beyond repair?

Make a list and talk with your sponsor, therapist, or support group about your thoughts. Prayerfully give the relationship to the God of your understanding. Remain open to the input you receive but remember that the final agreement is between you and the God of your understanding.

~ Task 4 ~

Which relationship do you need to avoid, if possible, because the relationship is too hurtful to you?

Make a list and talk with your sponsor, therapist, or spiritual advisor about strategies you can use to avoid harming others or getting hurt again yourself.

Chapter 6: An End to the Secrets – Step 5

One of the authors (the one who recently accepted his baldness) once proposed the elimination of the Fifth Step, as well as some of the others, because it was "a waste of time." The author in question (John) was barely two weeks sober and, after a thorough review of the 12 Steps, found that the whole program could be condensed into two steps: Step One (or at least the first half of it) and Step Twelve (minus the spiritual awakening). The Fifth Step, he rationalized, could be eliminated because he already knew what had happened. It was no one else's business. And if "God is everywhere and sees everything" as he had been taught as a child, there would be no need to report anything. The three-year reign of terror that resulted from his abbreviated step program won him the title of a "Two Step Commando" and made his life miserably ineffective. He would now-a-days support taking all Twelve Steps.

The first benefit of completing an honest Fifth Step will come in the form of the freedom you will experience from your transparency before the God of your understanding and another human being. The secrets we carry can become an unbearable burden that quickly lessens once the doors to our soul are opened. The person you have chosen for your confidant is apt to be able to help you manage the shame and guilt that, if left undisclosed, might trigger a return to the obsessive thinking that always preceded our harmful dependency. Your confidant can help to normalize some of the reactions you are having to the disclosure by relating personal identifications of their own story. Additionally, if the relationship develops, your confidant can help you remain accountable in the future.

Although the potential benefits are limitless, we will close with a promise that the quality of the spiritual awakening you began in the Third Step will be enhanced by your disclosure. Regardless of the nature of your relationship with a power greater than yourself, you will begin to experience an increased sense of spiritual and emotional awareness because of the giant step you have taken in the direction of being other-centered. When we are other-centered, it is a great deal easier to maintain the much-coveted "attitude of gratitude."

You are encouraged to share your Fourth Step in its entirety with the human recipient of your Fifth Step. You have prepared written material that will allow you to read it verbatim and avoid the potentially limiting tendency to ad-lib over the difficult parts. There may come a time where you want to share your Fifth Step with other members of your support system and perhaps even a loved one. Take counsel from others before you race off with your inventory in hand but in the end the ultimate decision is between you and the God of your understanding.

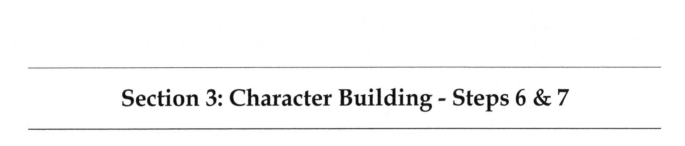

Section 3: Character Building - Steps 6 & 7

Chapter 1: The Forgotten Sixth and Seventh Steps

Those who have not forgotten the Sixth and Seventh Steps will attest to the vital role that they play in the development and maintenance of a sober life style. If you have forgotten these critical steps then you have suffered the consequences that have brought you to understand that true and lasting personality change is impossible without them. You have returned to these steps because you are tired of doing the same things over and over again expecting that the results are going to be different and desire the sanity promised in the Second Step. If you are approaching them for the first time you may see the challenge they represent as daunting. You may be confused about the true nature of your defects of character or how to develop the interventions you need in order to change the troublesome behaviors associated with them.

This guide will help you with both challenges. You can gain additional insights into yourself and what needs to be changed by discussing the steps with your support group, therapist, spiritual advisor, and in many cases a trusted family member. Get as much help as you need. You are worth it!

This guide is intended to provide you with an organized, task-by-task framework within which the Sixth and Seventh Steps can be completed in a meaningful way. When you have completed all the tasks you will have a clear and concise format for communicating your needs to others, and the areas in which fellowship support might be needed. Additionally, the task-focused design can be used again and again to monitor your ongoing progress after you have completed your initial Sixth Step.

The model used in this guide will focus your energy on the development of behavioral changes that can be objectively evaluated and modified as needed. The format will take you through the seven Tasks that you will find to be valuable aids in the identification and the replacement of the problematic behaviors that have become a part of your defects of character. Each of the Tasks is introduced with an in-depth discussion of its individual purpose and benefits you might desire. Directions for using the worksheets and an authors' sample for completing the worksheet in each task are also included for your reference.

It is hoped that you will explore only one defect of character at a time as you move through the first 6 Tasks. Task 7 should include all the defects you have written about as it represents your decision to go to the God of your understanding and ask that all your shortcomings be removed. Here is a summary of the seven Tasks for you to review before you begin writing.

Step-Sponsor Prompt

Stop

It is hoped that you will carefully read this entire section before beginning these seven Tasks.

Overview of the Sixth Step Tasks

Task 1: Naming the Defect

Give the defect of character a name or identify a phrase to describe the pattern of behaviors that you have developed for coping with uncomfortable emotions, situations, or people that you will ask to have removed by your higher power in the Seventh Step. Do not concern yourself with creating a name or title that will be universally accepted because that will probably be impossible. Seven different people will view the same behavior in seven different ways. A person's view of a behavior pattern or defect of character will be greatly influenced by his or her life experiences and the work that he or she has invested in his or her own personality change. The name you choose for the defect of character is not important. It is only important that you will be able to communicate to others what the defect means to you and why you have chosen it for removal. The answers to those questions will come to you as you work through the remaining Tasks.

Task 2: Identifying Common Symptoms

When most people begin to consider the job of addressing their defects of character they recoil from the perceived magnitude of the task. A thorough and searching inventory in the Fourth Step will have revealed many harms that we are responsible for. Since we are told that our wrongs are tied to our character defects we might wrongly assume that there will be hundreds or thousands of defects to address. Do not worry. Most of us will have but a handful of defects of character that present themselves as somewhat different from each other, depending upon the situation in which they surface. It only appears like there will be a huge list of shortcomings to address.

This Task will ask you to describe the common manifestations of each defect of character as it reveals itself in the various areas of your life; e.g., romantic relationships, work relationships, 12 Step meetings, school, etc. You may, for example, identify your "Problem with social anxiety" as one of the defects to address in your Sixth Step. The problem you have with social anxiety is likely to look different in a holiday family gathering then it will in a work presentation or entering a new 12 Step meeting for the first time. The Exhibit Snapshots provided in the pages to come will provide you with more guidance and direction.

Task 3: Reviewing the Bill

List the problems (costs) in your life, both past and present, which the defect has caused or worsened. This Task is not intended to be a repeat of your Fourth Step, but rather it is an exercise to lay down an outline of what the defect has cost you. It is intended to answer the questions:

- What has the behavior associated with my defect of character cost me in the past?
- What costs am I still paying in the present?
- What are the costs that I can expect to pay in the future if I do not take action?

The brief excavation exercise will direct your attention to many different types of costs and/or consequences that you or others have paid for the shortcoming you are examining. Your writing may resemble your approach to the First Step regarding your "drug of choice." When you first set out to chronicle the powerlessness and unmanageability in your life related to your progressive dependency on your "drug of choice" you were most likely directed to explore every area of your life for examples of powerlessness and unmanageability. You looked in the areas such as: social and familial relationships, financial management, physical and emotional health, spiritual well-being, legal problems and social status, and your personal feelings of worth and esteem. You will again be spanning the searchlight of recovery over the same territory but this time you are looking for the character defects that, if left unattended, could lead you back to your "drug of choice."

Task 4: Assessing the Payoff

This Task asks us to list the benefits derived, both past and present, from the defect under examination. Many of us are quick to say, "There are no benefits ... This defect is killing me and I would give anything to be rid of it." The defect of character that causes us the kind of pain that leaves us begging for immediate relief from the consequences is viewed by its host as intolerable and "any price" is considered fair to have it removed. However, the sufferer who is ready to have the darker and more consequential aspects of a character defect removed but feels entitled to hold onto those behaviors that seem to provide benefit without harm is going to miss the point of the Sixth and Seventh Steps. Let's revisit the wording of those steps again.

The Sixth Step reads: <u>Were entirely ready to have God remove all of these defects of character</u>. The Sixth Step author's choice of the words <u>entirely</u> and <u>all</u> would seem to make it clear that the intent was that we should engage in this Step without reservation or qualification that might allow us to retain certain aspects of our behaviors associated with a character defect. <u>Entirely</u> means complete disclosure and readiness and <u>all</u> means all. The Seventh Step reads: <u>Humbly asked Him to remove our shortcomings</u>. The choice of the word <u>humbly</u> suggests the method that we should follow in our request that our shortcomings or defects of character be removed. A humble request is presented with deference to the authority, power, or status of another in a way that honors the recipient. When we <u>humbly</u> ask God to remove our shortcomings we are acknowledging our lack of power or control over those defects and entrusting them to a Power greater than ourselves. We cannot entrust God with a part of the problem and hold onto those parts that are still generating benefit while hiding behind the rationalization that "nobody is perfect." If we are going to ask God to <u>remove our shortcomings</u> we are asking that God put an end to or to get rid of them. It would seem reasonable that we would be willing to let go of whatever we are asking God to get rid of. For many of us it is not always that clear though.

The gossiper whose assault on the character of another person who succumbs to the pressure of the smear campaign by attempting suicide will know great shame and regret. The behavior that is associated with character assassination seems ruinous at that level but many of us do not equate our behavior with that of someone who would really injure another. The scandalmonger is likely to draw the scorn of many and perhaps rightly so. But, what about the level of gossip intended to boost our sense of self worth or artificially elevate our status over the person whose character we are maligning? Is it really a defect in character when the target of the gossip is not aware of the attack or goes unharmed? Is there anything that needs to be removed? This level of gossip is felt by many to be harmless and very much a part of human nature. If the person is challenged about the behavior he is likely to become defensive as if some right of his was being infringed on. It does not stop here. There are many more levels we could examine but an in-depth review is outside the scope of this work. We suggest that while gossiping is a common defect of character it is not a feature of human nature. Instead we believe that it is a part of how humans can behave. We learn to be gossips and are not born that way. We believe that whatever we learn we can change. We eventually came to discover that there was no need to rationalize that we were only "being human" when we learned to replace the behavior associated with gossip with healthy strategies for coping with the social and emotional challenges we faced. Some of us will compartmentalize our life and behavior and conclude that whether or not we are "truly" gossiping depends on the circumstances.

Perhaps you have heard or supported the argument that public figures are fair game when it comes to gossip because they have chosen to have a public lifestyle or because they earn exorbitant incomes. The presidential candidate who opposes your views or the movie star that appears immoral are potential targets for the same defect of character - gossip that is capable of bringing about the horrible ends for the depressed person, noted above, who became the target of a smear campaign. This presentation of gossiping, which is seemingly more diluted and less consequential than the first three manifestations, is in reality no different. Gossiping is a defect of character whether we are discussing the relapse of a group member and it is all dressed up as "sharing and caring" or it is dark and sinister like the brand of gossip found in some political campaigns or divorce proceedings.

It has been said that it is easy to ask for the removal of those personality traits or behavioral patterns that are causing you harm. There is little courage or willingness required to ask to be rid of those coping strategies that cause pain with no gain. Who, for example, wants to run the risk of going to jail for robbing a bank? We know that the risk vs. reward ratio is way off, so most of us do not rob banks. Have you thought of cheating on your tax returns? If a friend offers you a slice of pizza from a restaurant they work at is that a problem for you? Is it stealing in the way that bank robbery or grand larceny is stealing? And what about stealing from stores? Retail theft is not even called stealing. When a thief steals from a store it is called shoplifting as if no one was being harmed. The shareholders of that store are being harmed. The customers, like you and me, are being harmed by the inflated prices we are charged to cover the cost of stolen goods. We have found that we have been better served by giving up the idea that there are different degrees of a defect of character. The practice of splitting hairs over whether or not one manifestation of a character defect is any more or less hazardous to our recovery is dangerous because it creates a very slippery slope. Whenever we defend our behavior by rationalizing that <u>it is not as bad as some greater</u> form of the wrong we should always add <u>YET</u>.

In order to bring the character defect to our higher power in the Seventh Step for removal we will need to have become ready as it indicates in the Sixth Step: <u>Were entirely ready to have God remove all of these defects of character</u>. The process of becoming ready is either a long and painful journey or it is a decision. If we decide that we are willing to have a defect of character removed we must be prepared to surrender the "good" with the bad. However, the Sixth Step is asking for more than the removal of a "cancerous tumor" from your personality.

But the reality is that there must be some way that you are benefitting from the behaviors associated with the defect or you would not continue to act in that way. The defect was developed in the past as a strategy for coping with some emotional discomfort, so there must be some current gain.

Task 5: The Things We Must Change

In this Task you are requested to identify the behaviors that you can eliminate that are related to the defect under examination. It is common to hear people rationalize their attack of another person's character by declaring that they don't seem to have any control over the impulse to judge others. Some will offer that their mean attack on others is being driven by some force outside of their own control like the "addict inside that is doing the talking for them or causing them to behave poorly." The only reason that our defects of character survive the healing that occurs in the first three steps is that we derive some payoff or benefit from the behavior associated with the defect. The defects that were not removed when we <u>made a decision to turn our will and our lives over to the care of God as we understood Him</u> remained because we enjoyed what certain aspects of the defects were still doing for us.

This Task is intended to pinpoint the specific behaviors that are associated with the defect of character that you are currently working on and would like to have removed. It is critical that the behaviors you recognize and mark for elimination are measurable. For example it is common to hear statements like: "I am going to stop being so angry." Anger is not a defect of character any more than love is a positive personality attribute. Angry is a feeling or a thought and is not an action like the verb hitting. Angry is an adjective whose function is to modify a noun or pronoun. <u>John is angry</u>. It describes how John appears or what he might be feeling but it does not tell us what he is doing. To understand what he is doing we have to watch his behavior. Let's take a closer look at angry John. <u>John was so angry that he hit himself in the knee cap with a sledge hammer</u>. The action of hitting himself with a hammer is the behavior associated with a defect of character that John has learned to use to handle his distress. I know your thinking that, "this guy has more problems than addiction," and you would be right but now is not the time to go into all that.

Labeling a feeling such as anger or an emotional state like resentfulness as being a character defect will leave you without direction on how to "ready" yourself for God to remove your shortcomings. To prepare for the surrender process found in the Seventh Step you will need to identify specific behaviors that you can discuss in detail and that others can observe once you have shared your Sixth Step with them. The Sixth Stepper who wants to give up the character defect which one might call "resentfulness" is going to be lost and unsure of where to begin. If, however, the resentfulness is examined for the specific behaviors that give voice or action to the emotional state then you can make changes that ready you for the Seventh Step. A brief illustration may illuminate the advantage to identifying explicit behaviors:

> John struggled for years with resentments that eventually haunted every aspect of his life. He had grown up in a chaotic and abusive alcoholic home and carried the resentments for the hurts he endured for years. In his step work he had developed a personal relationship with God and was working to clear away the wreckage of his past but resentment continued to dog him at every turn in his journey. When it came time to complete the Sixth Step he was clear that much would have to change. He was prepared to have a "spiritual surgery" - which is how he initially viewed the Seventh Step but did not know what to do. He understood that his resentfulness was robbing him of the freedom and happiness that he read were promised in the course of recovery.

His initial attempts at the Seventh Step were little more than prayerful pleadings or childlike efforts to magically wish certain aspects of his personality away. When he began to examine the specific ways in which his shortcomings manifested themselves through his behaviors the fog began to lift and he was no longer lost. He did not necessarily want to have all aspects of his character defects removed but he understood what they were. Instead of praying to have resentfulness removed he identified the behaviors that he came to understand as the outward demonstration of his shortcoming. In place of wishing away resentment he began to identify the ways he behaved when he was resentful. He found that he gossiped about people, mistreated anyone who reminded him of the wrongdoers from his past, and took direct and passive actions to prevent anyone from getting close enough to hurt him again. Here were behaviors that he could address in a proactive way to ready himself for God to remove his shortcomings.

It might be challenging at first to think in such precise ways about a defect of character but your efforts will be rewarded. You will discover, if you have not already, that it is not enough to say, "I am just not going to do it anymore," as most of us have tried that numerous times and in numerous areas in the past without relief. This Task will help you identify the behaviors that will have to be eliminated if you are to resist the lure of the defect of character.

Task 6: Replacement Behaviors

The behaviors that have been marked for elimination in Task 5 must be replaced with behavioral actions that will promote emotional health and spiritual wellbeing. This Task will help you to identify the behaviors you will need to introduce into your recovery plan in order to fill the "holes" created by those you are ready to give up to the God of your understanding. The question of whether or not to replace unhealthy coping strategies with sound methods for responding to the emotional challenges of life is not an option. It is a requirement for obtaining and maintaining emotional sobriety. If you can remember the withdrawal reaction you experienced when you were separated from your "drug of choice" then you will understand the importance of replacing a maladaptive coping strategy with a healthy one. The behaviors associated with our character imperfections had a "drug-like" quality to temporarily ease the pain of living.

If you once dealt with the fear of rejection by creating barriers between you and others, such as avoiding opportunities or refusing to share at Twelve Step meetings, then the removal of those behavioral avoidances will leave you feeling vulnerable and defenseless. The fear of rejection will need to be addressed in a proactive way with replacement behaviors for those you used to count on to create or maintain the illusion of safety. As an example, you could make a commitment to your sponsor and support group that you will raise your hand at the start of the opening discussion part of the meeting to share whatever is on your mind. This is a behavior that is observable and measurable if members of your support group are at the meeting. It is not hoping that you will be different. It is not trying to will the fear away. This replacement behavior would represent real and measureable change. These replacement behaviors represent some of the tools of sober living that make it difficult for the maladaptive patterns to take root should they begin to resurface.

Task 7: A Spiritual Offering

When you have completed Tasks 1 through 6 you will have a written profile from which you can discuss your character defects with others and a template from which to enact change needed to bring your recovery into <u>all your affairs.</u> Presenting your plan to the God of your understanding and another human being who will help you to monitor your progress along the way will provide you with a sobriety net that can catch you when you begin to stumble. We have often found that others were able to know that we were in trouble before we were aware. Sharing your Sixth Step with another human being will help to clarify for them what you look like when you are having difficulty and how they may be able to help. The other human being can be a sponsor, professional therapist, or a loved one. The more people you allow to know you, the more you will learn to know yourself.

Step-Sponsor Prompts

Prayer

God, I am preparing to embark on the Tasks that will guide me through the identification and replacement of the behaviors that I tried to use to buffer me from life. I wonder, at times, what I will be without my system of defenses but I trust that you have not brought me all this way to abandon me now.

Meditative Reflection

Imagine that you are at the beginning of a hike up a rocky slope. You have taken the steps needed to be physically, emotionally, and spiritually fit for the climb. You have been instructed on the preferred path to the top and have been coached on the proper use of your gear. You stand at the base of the hill and are struck with spikes of fear and doubt but you begin your ascent knowing that others have passed to safety on the trail that awaits you.

~ Task 1 ~

Naming the Defect

The name you assign to a defect of character does not matter all that much, as long as you do not confuse feelings with defects of character. Our feelings, whether they are comfortable like love and acceptance, or uncomfortable like anger and hurt, represent emotional sensations and not coping strategies. Anger is not a defect of character. The manner in which we cope with the feeling or behave when we are angry may contain a defect of character, but the feeling of anger is not, in itself, a defect any more than love or fear are character defects. The defects of character that have developed in our personalities have grown out of a desire to cope with an uncomfortable emotion such as anger, fear, or even love; but these feelings are not the problem. The ways in which we learned to cope with our feelings are the problem and the target of the Sixth and Seventh Steps.

Some recovery literature highlights the Seven Deadly Sins of pride, greed, anger, envy, sloth, gluttony, and lust when introducing the defects of character that we can examine during the course of undertaking a personal inventory. In our guides, we purposefully avoid issues of religion; therefore, we will not enter a discussion of the definition of "sin." Our only interest is in spiritual wellbeing, and we firmly believe that defects of character cut us off from the grace of the God of our understanding and generate conflicts in our relationships with others. If you prefer to use the deadly sins as a reference for your Sixth Step work, perhaps they will serve you. Our attempts to use the deadly sins as a reference for our Sixth Step work have not been helpful. They present harsh absolutes that, to us, were far too easy to dismiss as being traits of "really troubled souls." We unfortunately concluded that because we were "not that bad," we had no defects whatsoever once we had stopped our use of addictive substances or addictive behaviors.

We have since learned that our defects of character, no matter how mild when compared to our past behavior, will diminish our relationships with others, block our knowledge of God's will for us, and deprive us of the power of that will. We do not know whether or not God would view these behaviors as sins; that is for you to decide. We only ask that you begin by naming the defect.

We tried many other models of self-examination in an effort to give our defects of character a proper name because we thought it was vital to get the name correct. We were afraid of getting scolded by the "recovery police" who might interject: "That's not envy, it's fear…, "What is the matter with you anyway?" We spun our wheels for years before we decided that God would probably know our defects of character by any name or number we might give them. The real task in naming our defects was to form a profile that we could use to describe our inner workings to those whose help we were seeking. We needed to communicate problematic behavior patterns to others in a way that we would all understand. We settled on a simple model.

We give our defects of character a simple first name: "My problem," "with" (a middle name), and an "objective" (last name). As an example, when your struggle with the need to be in charge of everything causes you or others distress, the behaviors associated with the character defect are likely to appear as several different defects depending upon the environment in which the behavioral coping strategies surface. In a work environment you are likely to be viewed by some to be a micro-manager and others as an overbearing supervisor. A family member's description could vary depending on the nature of the relationship. A spouse might view you as a domineering "authoritarian," while a child could see an "overly protective dictator." 12 Step group members could dub you a "bleeding deacon" who always thinks he knows best and your neighbor will describe that they live next door to "psycho neat nick" whose yard has to have all the grass leaning in the same direction and who gets outraged when the leaves from other neighbor's trees land in his yard.

As you can see the name chosen to describe a character defect can have a great deal of variability. The disparate names given for the same behavior pattern can make a discussion of the behavior quite confusing. When the title that you and a sponsor would use to describe a character defect differs so significantly, e.g. "bleeding deacon" vs. "overly protective authoritarian," there is likely to be a huge communication problem. If you are trying to get help to intervene on a defect in your character that manifests itself in a variety of situations and in specific ways, it will not be helpful to waste time trying to agree on what it should be called.

As an example, instead of obsessing over whether or not the defect of character producing your "controlling" treatment of the people, events, and circumstances, is rooted in narcissism, grandiosity, or self-delusion you could simply call the defect "My problem with needing to be in charge of everything." My problem is the first name, needing to be in charge of everything is the last name, and with is the defect's middle name. You will have an opportunity to discuss the symptoms of that problem in Task 2. For now you just need to give the defect a name.

The realization that God speaks all languages freed us to focus our energy on the tougher aspects of the Sixth Step. We decided that our defects were to be given a simple first and last name; then we could get to work on the admission of the ways in which our defect of character manifests itself. The Naming the Defect Worksheet included in the Appendix will help you to organize your thoughts and create a profile of your defect to communicate to others.

Step-Sponsor Prompts

Think

In Exhibit 16, the authors present a sample Task 1: Naming the Defect worksheet with explanations of what is expected in each section. Please review it as well as the material above before moving on.

Snapshot

The following snapshot provides further explanation of the sub-tasks associated with Task 1: Naming the Defect. Each of the headings is intended to help you more fully communicate how your defect appears to you and how others might better understand what you are struggling with. When you are ready to complete Task 1 on your Sixth Step you will be directed to a blank sheet that contains the same bold-faced headings. Write your response in the area provided. This Snapshot is intended to explain to you what you are expected to examine under each heading.

Exhibit: 16
Title: Naming the Defect Worksheet
Subtitle: Described

The defect I am targeting is known to me as:

The name you give to the defect is not important. The defect's first name is "My problem." The defect's middle name is "with." The defect's last name is a behavioral descriptor or a feeling state, such as resentful or depressed. Do not choose a feeling like anger or love. Feelings are not defects of character. Defects of character are how we have learned to cope with our feelings like anger. With this example your defect's name would be: My problem with coping with anger.

My defect might be known by other names or phrases such as:

List terms that others might be more familiar with to describe your defect. The key purpose for Task 1 is to develop a picture of what your character defect represents to enable you to discuss the behaviors that are connected to it. If your sponsor or spouse will better understand your defect named: My problem with maintaining order if you were to call it procrastination or controlling then list those "nick names" here. Remember, it is not likely that your higher power will care what you call it.

If my defect were represented by an animal or a media character, it would be:

In an effort to bring dynamic life to your defect of character, choose the name of an animal or a cartoon or other media character that your support system might be able to better identify with. The animal or characterization you choose will provide others with a clearer understanding of how you behave under the influence of this defect. By choosing a cartoon character whose "personality" they are familiar with, you might have an easier time describing the behaviors that are causing you and others problems. The choice of an animal pseudonym for your character defect could also contribute meaning to the discussion. Of course, if your mentor is afraid of snakes it might not be a good idea to describe your problem with being possessive by describing yourself as a boa constrictor.

If my defect had a voice, it would say (about me):

Our defects of character can feed off of our resentments toward ourselves. Periods of internalized anger or resentment toward self can empower the "committee" in our heads to wage an assault against our self-esteem and sense of personal value that can leave us spiritually depleted and emotionally and socially ineffectual. The committee or singular voices in our head can be ruthlessly judgmental and the self-effacement can lead to a level of personal condemnation that precipitates estrangement from others and drains our gratitude for the moment and hope for the future. If your defect could talk what would it say to you about you? What names would your defect of character call you? How would it evaluate what you have as personal assets and support resources? What predictions would it have for your future? If your defect of character were titled: My problem with being possessive it may call you weak or a pathetic leech.

Exhibit: 16 (Continued)
Title: Naming the Defect Worksheet
Subtitle: Described

If my defect had a voice, it would say (about others):

Our defects of character can also feed off of the resentments we hold toward others. Our defects of character have the greatest impact on us through the way that they alter our relationships with others. Most of our shortcomings would lose form and disappear completely if we had no contact with others. We are not saying that our character defects are the responsibility of others or that other people push our buttons. We are not. We are saying that very few defects of character could survive without relationships. If you do not include defects that generate actual physical harm to you then it will be difficult to identify a defect to discuss in a Sixth Step that did not involve other people in some way.

Consider, for illustration purposes, that you are ship wrecked on a deserted island and contact with all other humans or animals is cut off forever. On a deserted island without relationships most of your defects of character would disappear. How many arguments have you had with another person about the difficultly you have with being on time? There would be nothing to be on time for and no one to be disappointed. If you struggle with gossip or envy who would know? There would not be arguments about laziness or hurt feelings associated with rejection. It would appear that we are designed to relate to others and our defects of character can make the task quite arduous if not impossible.

If your defect of character had a voice what names would it call others that might serve to alienate you from them? How would a talking defect of character describe the significant people in your life or portray the way that you are being treated by them? What does your defect of character suggest you should be thinking or feeling about others? If your character defect were titled: My problem with being possessive it might say that other people were unfaithful or unreliable. It might call them greedy, selfish, or untrustworthy.

Step-Sponsor Prompts

Snapshot

Do not rush into Task 1 just yet. The authors have prepared two samples of what Naming the Defect Worksheet might look like in Exhibit 17 & 18.

Think

The following Sample was chosen because it addresses the problem that many people have with coping with a feeling state. Please keep in mind that the defect of character is not "anger." Anger is not a defect of character anymore than the feelings of love or affection are defects of character. Anger is an emotion that has no inherent rightness or wrongness. Anger, love and affection do not cause problems. The problems that may develop from anger stem from the way that we cope with anger.

Exhibit: 17
Title: Naming the Defect Worksheet
Subtitle: Sample #1

The defect that I am targeting is known to me as:

My problem with coping with anger

My defect might be known by other names or phrases such as:

Peacemaker, spineless, shy (when I shut down while trying to cope with anger from others) bully, tyrant, and intimidator (when I take my anger out on others)

If my defect were represented by an animal, it would be a:

Clam, mouse, lamb (when I shut down while trying to cope with anger from others) and rabid dog, bull, T-Rex (when I take my anger out on others)

If my defect had a voice, it would say (about me):

You are so weak-willed it is no wonder that nobody likes you because you never take a stand. You are never going to amount to much if you let everyone push you around. How are you ever going to get ahead if you keep disappearing in the crowd (when I shut down while trying to cope with anger from others). You are really dangerous and it is probably best for all concerned if you stay by yourself. You knock people over with your overbearing presence and uncontrollable rampages. You see people as potential conquests and all you care about is what you can get from someone (when I take my anger out on others).

If my defect had a voice, it would say (about others):

If you come out of your shell and expose yourself everyone will know how incompetent you are. Everyone is out for their own gain and they don't care if you get stepped on. If you think you can handle yourself with them you are sadly mistaken - you will be eaten alive (when I shut down when trying to cope with anger from others). People are afraid of you because they are cowards. People don't really understand that you are a take-charge person because most are ashamed to admit that they are followers. Do not let people blame you for taking what they have failed to protect (when I take my anger out on others).

Step-Sponsor Prompt

Think

The following Sample introduces a defect that addresses an individual's problem with women and is not meant to suggest that the symptoms of sex or love addiction are really defects of character. The behaviors associated with sex or love addiction are not defects of character - they are symptoms of an addictive process. If you are a recovering sex/love addict this sample does not apply to you. It certainly may be advantageous for you to undertake a professional examination of your behavior to identify or rule out that you have a sex/love addiction. The sample is intended to address the phenomenon that is common for us when we find ourselves in conflict with a class of people or a type of institution. Many recovering substance addicted or food-addicted people will suffer from the defect used in the following Sample that are not sex/love addicted. The Sample could read: *My problem with authority figures* and as such would not be obscuring another diagnosis.

Exhibit: 18
Title: Naming the Defect Worksheet
Subtitle: Sample #2

The defect that I am targeting is known to me as:

My problem with women

My defect might be known by other names or phrases such as:

Womanizer, sexism, two-timer, pig, user, woman-hater, and cheat

If my defect were represented by an animal, it would be a:

Snake

If my defect had a voice, it would say (about me):

You are such a creep. You're just like your father.

If my defect had a voice, it would say (about others):

You cannot trust anybody. No one is safe. And they are all out to get something.

Step-Sponsor Prompts

Mentorship

If you are confused about where to begin with your defects of character consult with your sponsor, a member of your support group, your therapist, or a loved one to get input. Ask those you trust to identify the types of feelings, people, situations, or events that you have appeared to struggle with. If possible, confer with the recipient of your Fifth Step to see if there were particularly troublesome patterns to your behavior or the way that you interacted with life.

Action

Go to the Appendix G and complete Task 1 on the Naming the Defect Worksheet. This will be a profile on your first defect of character. There are six blank sheets. We limited the number of available sheets in order to encourage you to focus your attention on a limited number of defects. In Task 2, Identifying Common Symptoms, you will see that most of us have fewer defects than we think. The three to five defects most people have just present themselves in different ways, depending on the situation. If you need more sheets, you may make copies; but it is usually better to start with a manageable number of defects to work on and add others at a later time. If you select 10 different character defects to address you will greatly increase the monitoring efforts you will have to employ to make the intervention process meaningful.

Remember that your Sixth Step, like you, is a work in progress that will become more thorough with time. Start with the recommended three to five defects and add more later.

Think

Please complete Task 1 for only one defect and then go on to Task 2. Get to work! (Sorry. John made me say that.)

~ Task 2 ~

Identifying Common Symptoms

Many of us imagine that we have many more defects of character than we probably have. It appears in the beginning of our searching and fearless self-examination that our defects of character may number in the tens or hundreds. Do not be discouraged. The realistic number is probably closer to three or five, but it may seem to be many more. One of the reasons for this distortion in perception is that a particular defect of character may present itself in a variety of different ways, depending on the setting and the people involved. If a particular defect of character looks differently in different circumstances or with different people we are inclined to think that we have identified a unique shortcoming. It is also common for different people to describe or title the same character defect in different ways. If this happens with a confidant or support group member then you might be lead to believe that the two of you are talking about dissimilar deficiencies.

Let us illustrate this point. When addressing the defect named My problem with money, the defect might look like a completely different defect of character if it presents itself in the work setting versus in the company of my friends. In a work setting, My problem with money might look like low self-esteem because I continually compare my worth to the worth of my co-workers by comparing my salary to the salaries of others. In the company of my friends, My problem with money may take the form of pride as I brag about the things I have accumulated. This Task will help you to isolate the number of defects of character into a manageable number by guiding your work through listing the various symptoms of your defect in the key areas and relationships of your life.

When you undertake Task 2, we will ask you to scan the searchlight across the major areas of your life to identify the ways in which your defect presents itself. This Task, when completed, will guide you through the discussion of your defects with your sponsor or therapist. The Identifying Common Symptoms Worksheet included in Appendix H provides the following areas in which a defect could present itself with different symptoms:

- Work/school setting
- In the company of close friends
- In the company of extended family members
- In the company of my children
- In the company of my spouse
- In the company of my parents
- During sexual or romantic encounters
- While involved in 12 Step meetings
- When the management of finances is involved
- While involved in 12 Step work
- When dealing with the general public

All the areas may not apply to you, so feel free to use what you need and ignore the rest. If you identify an area or a manifestation that has not been listed, add it to your own sheet. The authors have supplied you with a sample of how the Identifying Common Symptoms Worksheet might be completed. Remember, you are working on only one defect at a time. The relationships and or the circumstances are going to be similar to the focal points of your Fourth Step inventory. You are not expected to rewrite your Fourth Step. It is not uncommon for our defects of character to surface in the same place that we might find the behavior associated with our active addictive processes. The space provided on the worksheet is intentionally restrictive to help you avoid long stories about your behavior that were already covered in your Fourth Step. If you begin rehashing the previous inventory's material, you will miss the intent of the Sixth Step.

Step-Sponsor Prompt

Snapshot

Please review the following two examples of Task 2 in Exhibit 19 and 20 that the authors prepared for you before beginning your own work.

Notes to Myself:

Exhibit: 19
Title: Identifying Common Symptoms Worksheet
Subtitle: Sample #1

Defect name:

My problem with coping with anger

Work/school setting:

When I was in elementary school, I was terrified of the other kids because it seemed to me that they were all so sure of themselves. The bullies were the worst. Anyone who could get other kids to make fun of me seemed to have tremendous power. The tough kids would challenge me or threaten to beat me up. When someone would come at me or talk to me in an angry tone I would freeze up inside and become very angry with myself because it seemed like the world that I could feel comfortable in grew smaller and smaller. I would generally find someone who was emotionally or physically weaker than me and I would make them the object of my fear by tormenting them physically or emotionally. In work settings as a young adult it was not uncommon for me to cope with my self-anger for not having learned a trade or furthered my education by cheating my employers out of the performance they were paying me for or in worse cases stealing from inventory of products or materials. As time progressed I would cope with my anger at missed opportunities or salary "injustices" by undermining the success of the operation in any way that I could.

In the company of close friends:

For many years my anger would manifest itself as cynicism or sarcasm with those I was closest to. I would tease them about their mistakes in an attempt to rob them of their joy or celebration of life because I was angry about something that was missing in mine.

In the company of extended family members:

The anger I felt for the abuses I experienced at the hands of the alcoholism that decimated my nuclear family often came out in many forms: harsh treatment, avoidance and isolation, character assassination, and attempts to slander the images that other people held for their parents. I did not consider that I was hurting anyone. I thought I was merely setting the record straight. My method for coping with the anger that I felt toward the wrongdoers in my life frequently took the form of my rejection of those who might genuinely care for me and try to love me. I thought that someone needed to pay for my hurt and no one should be happy if I was not.

In the company of my children:

My problem with coping with my anger would come out in a variety of ways in my relationship with my daughters and son. I sometimes coped with my anger at life by sulking and being emotionally unavailable for anyone even my children. If I were angry with some behavior of theirs, I might invoke the silent treatment or lecture them into an intellectual coma. I prided myself in never hitting them in anger but verbal disapproval could be equally as harsh as the physical abuse I had endured.

In the company of my spouse:

I handled my anger with my spouse by becoming critical and often unforgiving. The anger that I mismanaged outside of our relationship manifested itself in our marriage through unreasonable expectations and an inability to receive and process input from her without becoming argumentative and emotionally punishing.

Exhibit: 19 (Continued)
Title: Identifying Common Symptoms Worksheet
Subtitle: Sample #1

In the company of my parents:

I would cope with my anger towards my parents by avoiding them completely as an adult.

During sexual or romantic encounters:

My method for coping with my anger in sexual relationships was generally to avoid risking any emotional or physical intimacy. In romantic relationships my anger was never brought to the surface for resolution. I frequently terminated relationships by claiming the plight of the victim to cover up my anger with the dissatisfaction I felt in the relationship or with my life in general. I took great pride in never getting physically angry but the verbal tirades were often deafening not to mention the long periods of punishing avoidance.

While involved in 12 Step meetings:

My anger would seldom get expressed directly. My method for addressing anger showed itself in a variety of ways: I was an argumentative presence at business meetings, I rigidly and disrespectfully enforced the group's "conscience" decisions, openly challenged the misrepresentation of a recovery principle by another member or the misquoting of the literature as if I was the group parliamentarian.

When the management of finances is involved:

Hoarding money was one way of responding to my anger for never having "enough" in my life. I would sometimes appease my anger with an exorbitant purchase and argue later about the unstable nature of our finances. My anger with the "fortunate rich" took the form of character assassination and cheating others whenever I could.

While involved in 12 Step work:

My approach to coping with anger sometimes hurt those I might have been of some service to by depriving others of my time and failing to pursue opportunities to help those who I saw struggling in their recovery.

While dealing with the general public:

When dealing with the public I can be mean, egotistical, and argumentative. I drive too fast and accuse everyone else of being a dangerous driver. I easily become embroiled in political debates because I love getting the upper hand on my opponent. It does not much matter what the point is. I will usually take the opposing position to engage in a battle of words.

Exhibit: 20
Title: Identifying Common Symptoms Worksheet
Subtitle: Sample #2

Defect name:

My problem with women

Work/school setting:

When I was in school, I was terrified of girls and I would spread rumors about sexual conquests that were not true in an attempt to inflate my image and self-esteem. By the time I graduated from high school, I viewed women largely as objects. Every relationship was a game of chase-and-conquer. In the work environment, competent women would easily threaten me and I would work to undermine their success through gossip and flirtation.

In the company of close friends:

When I am with my friends I talk about women in a way that is disrespectful. The jokes will be highly sexual and sexist. I will talk about women as if they were nothing more than a collection of body parts.

In the company of extended family members:

The members of my family took vicarious pride in the romantic and sexual accomplishments of others and welcomed my dating stories regardless of whether they were fancied or real. I would hang with the men and allow women to assume the responsibility for the tasks associated with a particular event. I knew nothing about being a romantic couple around family. My girlfriends and adult romantic partners were prizes to show off.

In the company of my children:

My children have watched me argue with and berate my wife. They have observed vulgar name-calling. They have seen me treat my wife as if her purpose in life were to serve me and make me happy.

In the company of my spouse:

I have flirted with women in the presence of my wife and when she would confront me about it later, I would tell her that she was crazy and obviously not feeling very secure with herself. I watch other women's bodies and declare, "There is no harm in looking at the menu as long as you don't order."

In the company of my parents:

I would behave in a domineering manner toward women when I was around my parents because I wanted them to perceive me as being in control.

During sexual or romantic encounters:

Romantic encounters never involved openness or intimacy. I was always falling into love for the relationship's potential. I was incapable of making a commitment and generally made it look as if the breakup was the woman's fault. In sexual matters, fantasy ruled the event. I was seldom emotionally present and frequently found myself fantasizing about other women. I was unfaithful at every opportunity, but demanded complete fidelity from my partners.

Exhibit: 20 (Continued)
Title: Identifying Common Symptoms Worksheet
Subtitle: Sample #2

While involved in 12 Step meetings:

In 12 Step meetings, I was always on the prowl. I ignored the unspoken rules about staying away from the newcomers and frequently lured prospective partners into my grasp with the bait of "sincere fellowship." I used meetings to meet women and chose topics of discussion to convince my targets that I was truly sober.

When the management of finances is involved:

I frequently mismanaged money and blamed my partners for their overindulgence. I welcomed gifts and gave few. Money was a way to control women. If she had more, I made her feel bad about it. And if I had more, I used it to induce insecurity in her.

While involved in 12 Step work:

My 12 Step work, where women were concerned, was really 13th Step work all dressed up as sharing and caring. I would flirt with the wives and partners of men I was supposed to be guiding.

While dealing with the general public:

In public I would present myself in any way that would attract the opposite sex. There were no rules.

Step-Sponsor Prompts

Prayer

God help me to remain focused on the task at hand. I find myself drifting back to the wrongs I identified in my Fourth Step and I do not want to begin feeling hopeless. I know that there is much that I will need to do to repair the damage I have done, but I trust that you have not brought me this far to leave me on my own.

Meditative Reflection

Imagine that you have completed your Eighth Step and you are waiting for the opportunity to make amends. You are standing before the people or institutions you have wronged, prepared to acknowledge your wrongs and to describe the defects of character that have led to your hurtful behavior. Watch them closely. Their faces will communicate that you are being seen as humble, sincere, and knowledgeable. They can be sure of your commitment to change because you are able to describe the dynamic nature of your hurtful behavior. You cannot change what you do not understand. Your work through the Sixth and Seventh Steps will help you to gain that understanding.

Action

Go to Appendix H and complete Task 2 on the Identifying Common Symptoms Worksheet. There are six blank sheets. We limited the number of available sheets in order to encourage you to focus your attention on a limited number of defects. If you need more sheets you may make copies, but please do not distribute them to others. Please avoid the tendency to retell the stories of your Fourth Step because it will take you off course.

Think

Task 3: Reviewing the Bill Worksheet will initially appear to be a restatement of your Fourth Step inventory, but it is not. The close examination of your defects of character that you have undertaken would not bare much fruit if you could not develop specific plans for changing the problematic behaviors associated with the defect. Task 3: Reviewing the Bill Worksheet and Task 4: Assessing the Payoff Worksheet are essential to identifying the behaviors that you will need to eliminate and what the replacement behaviors will be. Get back to work before you end up writing about procrastination or avoidance as defects. Only kidding! We are with you in spirit, but you have to do the work.

~ Task 3 ~

Reviewing the Bill

The defects of our character are made up of a series of behaviors that were designed to keep us safe from harm, but now those behaviors only cause harm. The first step toward identifying the behaviors that must be eliminated is to be clear about what the behaviors associated with the defect of character have cost us. If you realize that a particular behavior is causing harm to you or to someone you care for, and that knowledge does not prevent the recurrence of that behavior, then the behavior is tied to a defect in your character. Do not fool yourself by calling it a bad habit.

The Seventh Step is where we make the change in our attitude that permits us, with humility as our guide, to move out from ourselves in service to God and our fellows. Recovery meeting discussions of the Seventh Step often focus on humility. It is understandable that a review of the literature would lead to a discussion of the dynamics of the development of humility; however, the practice of the Seventh Step requires much more than a humble willingness to change. The development of the quality of humility is vital to all spiritual progress because it helps us to align our behavior with the knowledge of God's will for us. The Seventh Step opens the gateway to vast spiritual development. Passage through that gateway requires that we pay the entrance fee, or bill, if you will. Our payment will come in Task 5 when we begin the preparation of our offering of behavioral change for God's review in the Seventh Step. We must first understand what we owe before we can develop an appropriate payment plan or plan for behavior changes.

The defects of our character are likely to have cost us plenty. Completing the following Reviewing the Bill Worksheet can tally the price tag for both past and present behaviors.

Step-Sponsor Prompt

Snapshot

In Exhibit 21 the authors introduce you to the format to be used for Reviewing the Bill Worksheet along with explanations of what is expected in each section. Please review the model as well as the material above before moving on.

Exhibit: 21
Title: Reviewing the Bill Worksheet
Subtitle: Format

Defect: My problem with …			
Area & Items	**Past**	**Now**	**Long-Term Impact/Future Cost**
Sex/Romance	▨	▨	▨
Money/Material Possessions	▨	▨	▨
Emotional Security	▨	▨	▨
Power/ Status	▨	▨	▨

Area & Items

Reviewing the Bill Worksheet provides space for you to itemize the costs of the defect of character you are exploring. The column entitled "Area & Items" provides space for you to describe briefly the specific costs that you have paid or are paying for the behaviors associated with a defect of character. The cost we experience will take a variety of forms. Cost can be financial, social, emotional, spiritual, physical, legal, etc. The cost items you identify can be related to those you have endured as well as those experienced by others on whom your defect of character or the behaviors associated with it have made an impact.   The areas of concentration: Sex/Romance, Money/Material Possessions, Emotional Security, and Power/Status are thought to be the major areas of our life that our defects of character develop in order to cope with discomfort or unmet needs.

Exhibits 22 and 23 will present samples of the Reviewing the Bill Worksheet the authors have completed on the defect titled *My Problem with Coping with Anger* and *My Problem with Women* respectively. Reviewing the Bill Worksheets that you will be working from will include a number of choices that are common costs reported by recovering people that may apply to the defect you are examining. The Samples used in Exhibits 22 and 23 do not include all the choices. You are encouraged to add your personal items in the worksheet that appears in Appendix I.

Exhibit: 21 (Continued)
Title: Reviewing the Bill Worksheet
Subtitle: Format

Past and Now

The columns "Past" and "Now" provide space for you to identify whether the cost item has been incurred in the past, is currently being incurred, or both. Place a check in the past column if the cost was incurred in the past. Place a check in the "Now" column if you are still experiencing the cost.

Long-Term Impact/Future Cost

The column titled "Long-Term Impact/Future Cost" provides space to describe briefly the long-term impact that the defect has had on you and/or what you believe the future cost might be if you do not change.

Long-term impact is meant to have you examine the cumulative impact of a specific aspect of the defect of character. This broad view of the impact of your behavior is important because it is easy for us to underestimate the cost that our behavior has had on others. We tend to see our behavior as isolated incidents while others experience them as "here we go again" patterns. It is also important to consider what the future costs might be if you are unwilling to make the behavioral changes needed in Tasks 5 and 6.

Please review the examples of Task 3: Reviewing the Bill Worksheet that we prepared for you before you begin your own work.

Step-Sponsor Prompt

Snapshot

In Exhibit 22 the authors present the first of two samples for Task 3: Reviewing the Bill Worksheet that addresses a review of the costs associated with the behaviors the individual used/uses to cope with the feeling of anger. Please review the two samples before moving on or beginning Task 3.

Exhibit: 22
Title: Reviewing the Bill Worksheet
Subtitle: Sample #1

Defect: My problem with coping with anger			
Area & Items	**Past**	**Now**	**Long-Term Impact/Future Cost**
Sex/Romance			
Unresolved anger created deep conflict	X		I have many injured relationships to repair
Sarcastic communication with injured romantic partners		X	Communication deficits will leave me alone
Displays of anger compromised partner safety	X		
Bitter exchanges with romantic partners made physical intimacy difficult	X	X	I risk missing out on physical love
Angry/rageful behavior contributed to one divorce and is threatening current marriage	X	X	I may lose marriage
Money/Material Possessions			
Trouble with anger triggers impulse spending	X	X	Spending beyond my means increased debt
Anger with authority figures increased workplace problems & threatening job security	X		
Angry outbursts lead to mishandling of home equipment	X		
I had to replace or do without damaged possessions	X		
Road rage has cost several fines and contributed to auto accidents	X		I am still dealing with an outrageous insurance rate
Emotional Security			
My method of coping with anger drives people I care about away from me	X	X	I could end up as lonely as when I was active in my addiction
Bouts of unresolved anger and resentment generate/exacerbate my depression	X	X	My depression robs me of faith and hope
Angry overeating contributes to painful mood swings	X		
Power/ Status			
Anger creates dangerous sense of omnipotence	X		
Unresolved anger and resentment can diminish my ability to remain logical and rational	X	X	If I do not change my personality I will continue to lose friends
Angry demeanor led to loss of status in the workplace and community	X		
Brooding anger has lessened my esteem in my family	X	X	I have many amends to make to the people in my family

---

Step-Sponsor Prompt

Snapshot

In Exhibit 23 the authors present the second sample for Reviewing the Bill Worksheet that addresses a review of the costs associated with the behaviors the individual used/uses to cope with women. If you are recovering from sex addiction please refer to the Step-Sponsor Prompt Think that appears on page 80 for additional guidance. Please review the two samples before beginning Task 3.

Notes to Myself:

Exhibit: 23
Title: **Reviewing the Bill Worksheet**
Subtitle: Sample #2

Defect: My problem with women			
Area & Items	**Past**	**Now**	**Long-Term Impact/Future Cost**
Sex/Romance			
Caused those I cared for to feel less about themselves	X		Romantic partners felt used by me and I have come to feel dirty & unlovable as a result
Caused those I cared for to pull away from me	X		Family and friends have been hurt by the way I have treated women and they pull away from me
Left me sexually unfulfilled	X	X	I never felt satisfied & I still have a hard time remaining present with my partner
Money/Material Possessions			
Spent a great deal of money trying to impress women	X		I struggle to make emotional investments in romantic relationship since I stopped buying "love"
Gave away huge sums of money to buy my way out of relationships	X		Don't have adequate retirement funds
Failed to increase my income in my job because of promotional opportunities that were denied me because of my behavior	X		Don't have adequate retirement funds and can not afford desired vacations
Emotional Security			
Created distance between me and my higher power	X	X	I spent a great deal of time feeling ashamed of myself and today I find prayer difficult
Lowered my self-image	X		I suffer/ed periods of great depression
Evaporated hope that I had/have for the future	X	X	I have difficulty maintaining hope that I can change
Cause/d me to experience periods of loneliness	X	X	I have known dark, lonely periods & I can still feel all alone in a room full of people
Power/ Status			
Diminished my job performance	X		Flirtation was a distraction on the job and work performance suffered
Darkened my image with people that mattered to me	X		I suspect my partner would reject me if she knew other females saw me as a "user"
Lead to a relapse in my primary addiction	X		Many times when wanting to deaden the pain has caused me to relapse

---

Step-Sponsor Prompt

Action

Go to Appendix I and complete Reviewing the Bill Worksheet. There are six blank sheets. We limited the number of available sheets in order to encourage you to focus your attention on a limited number of defects. If you need more space attach loose-leaf sheets.

~ Task 4 ~

Assessing the Payoff

Our defects of character began as coping strategies for dealing with the feelings associated with difficult situations and challenging people. In the beginning they were assets and not liabilities. In order for you to identify the behaviors that will need to be eliminated in Task 5: The Things We Must Change, or replaced in Task 6: Replacement Behaviors, you will need to understand the present and past benefits that you derive or have derived from the behaviors associated with the defect you are examining.

Most of us struggle with this Task because we have difficulty seeing beyond the problems that the defect of character has caused or is still causing. The reality is that the defects of character that appear to be the most resistant to change are the ones from which we are still deriving some benefit. We will not be able to change the behaviors that are tied to the defect if those behaviors are still doing something for us. What the behaviors did for you or what those behaviors are still doing for you is called "the payoff."

We do not believe that people suffering with addictive illnesses are inherently bad people. We believe that addictive illnesses are real disease entities that have identifiable symptoms, follow predictable courses of progression, develop chronic patterns of maladaptive behavior, diminish the physical, emotional, and spiritual quality of the sufferer's life, and can be arrested through the development of a comprehensive plan for recovery. Unfortunately for the sufferer, addictive illnesses employ their victims as allies and those of us who have been victims are generally the last to know that we are ill.

Equally unfortunate for those afflicted with addictive illnesses is the shroud of shame that still hangs over the admission of a problem. Public perception of those suffering from substance-based addictive illnesses have improved in the past thirty years, but they are still largely viewed as suffering from an illness that is "self-inflicted." Public awareness and support for the treatment of sexual addiction is beginning to emerge, but it is many years behind the awareness and support for the treatment of alcoholism.

Addicted people are blamed for the choices they make while others suffering from chronic, progressive, and potentially fatal illnesses are seen primarily as victims. The heart attack victim may have aided and abetted his illness through poor diet, a lack of exercise, smoking, an excessive life style, etc. (all choices), but he is not blamed for having heart disease. The chronic diabetic may choose the same unhealthy lifestyle as the heart attack victim, thereby sacrificing a great deal of the quality of his life, but is not blamed for causing the disease or the problems that stem from it.

The addicted person, like the heart disease sufferer and the diabetic, will have to examine his or her choices if sustained recovery is going to be possible. Task 4, Assessing The Payoff of your defects of character will help reduce the likelihood of relapse and will improve the quality of your recovery. Of course, there is going to have to be sacrifice, but that is all right because most of us have already gotten more than our share of free rides.

Step-Sponsor Prompts

Think

The Assessing the Payoff Worksheet found in the Appendix J will help you to identify the potential benefits from the defect that may have served to strengthen this defect in the past or continue to make it difficult for you to address it today. The task is vital because you will not be able to develop a plan for behavioral change in Tasks 5 and 6 without the knowledge of what you will have to give up.

Snapshot

In Exhibit 24 the authors introduce you to the format to be used for Assessing the Payoff Worksheet along with explanations of what is expected in each section. Please review the model as well as the material above before moving on.

Exhibit: 24
Title: Assessing the Payoff Worksheet
Subtitle: Format

Defect: My problem with ...		
Benefit/Payoff	**Past**	**Now**
Sex/Romance	▨	▨
Money/Material Possessions	▨	▨
Emotional Security	▨	▨
Power/ Status	▨	▨

Format

The Assessing the Payoff Worksheet is broken down into four general areas of potential benefit: Sex/Romance, Money/Material Possessions, Emotional Security, and Power/Status with references to whether or not the benefits are identifiable in the past, now, or both.

Benefit

A benefit, as defined for the purpose of the guide, refers to something that represents a desired effect. One person's benefit may appear to another as a deficit. A "benefit" is something that your character defect or the associated behaviors of that defect are doing for you. It may be that it allows you to avoid a discomfort that was once viewed as an asset. If you continually get stuck with this issue, focus on the fact that addicted or co-addicted people are generally not doing what they are doing because they desire pain. Your defect brought you or is still bringing you some benefit or else you would not be engaging in the behaviors.

Past

Check this box if the benefit was present in the past even though you may no longer be engaged in the behaviors that caused you difficulty.

Now

Check this box if the benefit is still present in your life even if you are no longer as bad as you used to be. You may be able to check both "Past" and "Now."

The first column, titled "Benefits," provides examples of commonly reported payoffs for behavior associated with various defects of character. The examples have been placed under the heading that the authors believe represent the best fit. You are encouraged to add your personal entries on the blank worksheets, found in the Appendices, and place them under whichever heading seems to fit.

Columns two and three titled "Past" and "Now," respectively, provide space for you to identify those benefits that you have derived in both the past and present. Place a check in the "Past" column if the benefit was gained in the past. Place a check in the "Now" column if you are currently benefiting from the defect.

Step-Sponsor Prompt

Snapshot

In Exhibit 25 the authors present the first of two samples for Assessing the Payoff Worksheet that addresses a review of the past/present benefits/payoffs of the behaviors associated with the defect of character under examination. This sample deals with an individual problem with coping with the feeling of anger. Please review the two samples before beginning Task 4.

Exhibit: 25
Title: Assessing the Payoff Worksheet
Subtitle: Sample #1

Defect: My problem with coping with anger		
Benefit/Payoff	**Past**	**Now**
Sex/Romance		
I would/will use my anger to pick a fight with my partner to avoid sexual contact	X	X
I would use my anger to justify treating members of the opposite sex as objects	X	
Unresolved anger would dismantle a romantic relationship allowing me to avoid working honestly on the problems	X	
Money/Material Possessions		
I would use my anger at the "sins" of the wealthy to justify my own dishonest behavior	X	X
When I was angry I would hoard money or food	X	
Angry episodes would be/are quelled with impulse spending	X	X
Emotional Security		
My emotional insecurity would be/is obscured by my anger	X	X
When I was angry I have and still do blame others for my emotional insecurity allowing me to avoid examination of the root cause	X	X
Power/ Status		
Angry people are perceived by others as being powerful	X	
When people were /are afraid of my anger I generally got my own way	X	X
I used my anger to convince people that I was more capable than I was	X	
I use /d my anger to put others down in an effort to elevate my status	X	X

Step-Sponsor Prompt

Snapshot

In Exhibit 26 the authors present the second sample for Assessing the Payoff Worksheet that addresses a review of the past/present benefits/payoffs of the behaviors the individual used/uses to cope with women. If you are recovering from sex addiction please refer to the Step-Sponsor Prompt Think that appears on page 80 for additional guidance. Please review the two samples before beginning Task 4.

Exhibit: 26
Title: Assessing the Payoff Worksheet
Subtitle: Sample #2

Defect: My problem with women		

Benefit/Payoff	Past	Now
Sex/Romance		
Allows me to flirt without having to reveal all of myself	X	X
Allusiveness keeps others interested in me	X	X
Helps me to avoid sexual intimacy and risk	X	X
Makes the other person responsible for how sexual or vulnerable I become	X	X
Creates the illusion of a perfect mate through fantasy	X	X
Makes other men think I am better than they are	X	X
My flirtation causes my current partner to try & please me more	X	X
I don't have to compare my abilities to the abilities of women if I compromise them through seduction	X	X
Money/Material Possessions		
Helps me to obtain things I believe that I need	X	
Allows me to justify taking what belongs to others	X	X
Gives me a way of taking more than my fair share	X	X
Prevents others from taking my stuff	X	
I walked away from romantic relationships with material possessions my partners and I purchased together	X	
Manipulated partners into buying me peace-keeping gifts	X	
Emotional Security		
Allows me to hide my true feelings from others	X	X
Helps to calm my internal agitation	X	X
Keeps others from getting to know me	X	X
Enables me to blame others for the quality of my life & promotes others to feel indebted to me	X	X
Deadens my feelings	X	X
I do not have to take a risk to be hurt by anyone	X	X
If my partners remain insecure, then I can feel superior	X	
I can keep several prospects on my injured reserved list in case I am lonely or bored	X	
Power/ Status		
Leaves me feeling superior to others	X	
Leads others to be afraid of me	X	
Promotes others to feel less than and dependent on me	X	
I can feel energized by the contest for affection	X	

Step-Sponsor Prompt

Action

Go to Appendix J and complete Assessing the Payoff Worksheet. There are six blank sheets. We limited the number of available sheets in order to encourage you to focus your attention on a limited number of defects. If you need more space attach loose-leaf sheets.

Notes to Myself:

~ Task 5 ~

Things We Must Change

The defects in our character that are no longer haunting us will appear to be easy to offer up to God in the Seventh Step; but a comprehensive Sixth Step may be more involved than you might have first thought.

We are likely to experience an internal civil war when we commence to reframe our personality and give up the harmful behaviors associated with our defects of character. Honest and intimate relationships require significant risk. The fear that can be generated will often awaken defects that, while they appeared to be gone, were in reality only sleeping.

Do not assume that, because a defect of character does not appear to be active, the urge to return to your old ways will not challenge you in the future. In fact, you should expect that your inactive defects are like sleeping tigers that wake up hungry when you begin your Sixth Step work. Our defects of character seem to have a life of their own that will be disturbed when they are challenged. Do not be surprised to find yourself experiencing increased irritability when you probe the patterns of your past and present behaviors. Your defects will appear to resist inspection and retaliate when you try to remove the vehicles of their expression, which are your problematic behaviors.

Additionally, it is hazardous to assume that a particular defect of character is not producing any benefit and therefore there are no behaviors that can be eliminated. If you are still struggling with a defect of character that appears resistant to change, then you are still getting some benefit from the behaviors associated with that defect. We generally do not behave in a certain way because it generates pain. We are looking to feel better and not worse. Some might argue that their behavior is intentionally self-destructive and serves no benefit. To demonstrate, let us illustrate the basis for this belief with one of our own patterns (it is really John's, but he did not want us to say).

"During the end of my active alcoholism, I would be filled with such emotional pain that the thought of suicide was an almost constant companion. During that same period, it would not be uncommon to find me in the San Juan café in the inner city neighborhood of my youth. It would be about midnight when I would, as the establishment's only non-Spanish speaking patron, begin to yell the only Spanish that I knew: the curse words. The evening would end with a horrific beating with me as the guest of honor. It would hurt like hell but it would also serve as a cleansing. The pain on the outside of me (and there was plenty of it) was now greater than the pain on the inside of me. I felt better with a beating. My behavior, however self-destructive, returned the desired benefit. It may have looked like a desire to bring on pain but it was, in fact, a plan for numbing my emotional pain."

To those who hold to the idea that the behaviors associated with a defect of character are not doing anything for them, we suggest that you deny yourself the behaviors in question and watch what happens. If you eliminate the behaviors associated with a defect of character <u>in all your affairs</u> you are likely to develop a craving for those behaviors. If left unaddressed, the level of craving will begin to approach the desire you once knew for your drug of choice. These are mood-altering behaviors that must be replaced with healthy coping strategies if relapse is to be avoided.

Step-Sponsor Prompt

Snapshot

In Exhibit 27 the authors introduce you to the format to be used for The Things We Must Change Worksheet along with explanations of what is expected in each section. Please review the model as well as the material above before moving on. The Things We Must Change Worksheet will provide you with a framework within which you can categorize the behaviors that you will have to eliminate or change.

Exhibit: 27
Title: The Things We Must Change Worksheet
Subtitle: Format

Defect: My problem with...		
Behaviors to Eliminate/Change	**Now**	**Plan**
Sex/Romance	▨	▨
Money/Material Possessions	▨	▨
Emotional Security	▨	▨
Power/ Status	▨	▨

Behaviors to Eliminate/Change

The first column titled "Behaviors to Eliminate/Change" provides examples of commonly reported behaviors to eliminate or changes to be made that are associated with a variety of different defects of character. The examples have been placed under the heading that the authors believe represents the best fit. You are encouraged to add your own personal additions in the space provided.

The areas of concentration: Sex/Romance, Money/Material Possessions, Emotional Security and Power/Status are thought to be the major areas of our life that defects of character develop to cope with discomfort or unmet needs.

Exhibits 28 and 29 present samples of The Things We Must Change Worksheet the authors have completed on the defect titled "My Problem with Coping with Anger" and "My Problem with Women" respectively. The Things We Must Change Worksheets that you will be working from will include a number of choices that are common behaviors to eliminate or change, reported by recovering people, that may apply to the defect you are examining.

Exhibit: 27 (Continued)
Title: The Things We Must Change Worksheet
Subtitle: Format

Now

Columns two and three titled "Now" and "Plan," respectively provide space for you to check those behaviors that need to be eliminated or changed. Place a check in the "Now" column if you have already initiated a change for the behavior.

Plan

Place a check in the "Plan" column if you plan on making a change in that behavior.

Step-Sponsor Prompt

Snapshot

In Exhibit 28 the authors present the first of two samples for The Things We Must Change Worksheet that addresses the identification of behaviors to be eliminated that are associated with the defect of character under examination. This sample deals with an individual problem with coping with the feeling of anger. Please review the two samples before moving beginning Task 5.

Exhibit: 28
Title: The Things We Must Change Worksheet
Subtitle: Sample #1

Defect: My problem with coping with anger		
Behaviors to Eliminate/Change	**Now**	**Plan**
Sex/Romance		
I will make sure that I have my partner's consent before giving any input		X
I will not allow myself to go for more than 24 hours before I share my feelings with my partner	X	X
Money/Material Possessions		
I will not spend money when I am upset unless a bill has to be paid		X
I will not read newspaper articles or watch news that concentrates on the financial mismanagement or dishonesty of others and not engage in discussion about economics	X	X
Emotional Security		
I will not eat when I am angry		X
I will eliminate gossip from my communication and not listen to it from others	X	X
I will not blame others for how I am feeling		X
Power/ Status		
I will not participate in discussions about religion or politics	X	X
I will not participate in 12 Step business meetings that become heated		X
I will not attempt to convince anyone of my position on any issue	X	X

Step-Sponsor Prompt

Snapshot

In Exhibit 29 the authors present the second sample for The Things We Must Change Worksheet that addresses the identification of behaviors to be eliminated that are associated with the defect of character under examination. This sample deals with an individual who has problems with women. If you are recovering from sex addiction please refer to the Step-Sponsor Prompt Think that appears on page 80 for additional guidance. Please review the two samples before moving on or beginning Task 5.

Exhibit: 29
Title: The Things We Must Change Worksheet
Subtitle: Sample #2

Behaviors to Eliminate/Change	Now	Plan
Defect: My problem with women		
Sex/Romance		
Refrain from flirting with anyone but my partner in a committed relationship		X
Refrain from allowing anyone but a partner in a committed relationship to flirt with me		X
Refrain from the use of solitary masturbation		X
Refrain from the use of solitary pornography		X
Avoid conversations that objectify members of the opposite sex	X	
Abstain from sex outside my marriage	X	
Money/Material Possessions		
Avoid giving gifts to express emotions that have not been verbally shared		X
Emotional Security		
No longer pretend to be comfortable when I am uncomfortable	X	
Stop telling people what I think they want to hear		X
Refuse to participate in or listen to gossip even if it is called "caring and sharing"	X	
Stop blaming the quality of my life on those who hurt me		X
Avoid the use of mood-altering substances including foods which have a mood-altering effect on me	X	
Avoid situations which will allow me to isolate from others unless it has a specific spiritual focus		X
Do not allow women to flirt with me		X
Power/ Status		
Refrain from giving others unsolicited input		X
Do not focus on the shortcomings of others		X
Do nothing to undermine the success of others	X	

Step-Sponsor Prompt

Action

Go to Appendix K and complete The Things We Must Change Worksheet. There are six blank sheets. We limited the number of available sheets in order to encourage you to focus your attention on a limited number of defects. If you need more space attach loose-leaf sheets.

∼ Task 6 ∼

Replacement Behaviors

Many of our defects of character have become such an intricate part of our daily lives that we may not be aware of the degree of our dependency on them. As you continue working on the Sixth and Seventh Steps you will hear your defects groan and squeal as they resist removal. During this time of cleansing, service to others can be invaluable. Equally important as service, is the need to replace the old coping strategies with new healthy ways of coping.

In the beginning, the replacement behaviors will seem like nothing more than attempts to move out of harm's way. You will eventually come to understand that these new behaviors are filling the emotional and spiritual holes created when the unhealthy behaviors are eliminated. At first it will seem as if there is little you can actually do without the behaviors that have helped in the past to fill the void in you, however, you are not defenseless without your defective behaviors. In fact, their elimination will make room for the God of your understanding to take up residence. Have faith, for you will not be left to the fate of the "hole in the doughnut" for long.

Most of us have made reactive changes when the consequences of our behavior hurt too much. Reactive changes are usually instituted shortly after some behavior of ours has caused others harm or when we have gotten into trouble and have been told "there will be a price to pay." The changes we made were generally immature responses that are narrow in focus and childlike in nature. One of the authors (see if you can guess who) once sought out admission to a seminary to become a priest after a romantic interest threatened to kill herself upon discovery that the author had been unfaithful again. The solution to join the priesthood was self-punishment for "being immoral" and was motivated by fear. The entrance into the priesthood was intended to deny the wrongdoer of future sexual pleasures for his recent "indiscretion." The fear-based nature of this planned retreat was related to the perception that it would only be through complete abstinence that the immoral nature of his personality would be controlled.

Reactive changes are usually ineffective and short-lived. They were designed to numb the burning pain of guilt and were not designed to address the defect of character. Knee-jerk changes of this kind do not last long because the pain subsides and we rationalize that we had made a "rash decision" and "simply need to control our urges". If we are ever going to change our personalities, we need to consider proactive changes that will be lasting.

Proactive changes are intended to address the needs or challenges that we face in our day-to-day lives, as well as the origins of our defects of character. All of us experience the need for sex and romantic love, the need to provide for the material essentials of life, and to obtain some of the creature comforts. Each of us understands the importance of maintaining emotional security because ongoing change is virtually impossible without it. Additionally, it is common to desire status in society and to be important to our family, friends, and the larger community of our fellows. We suspect that humanity has always had these basic needs. The problem does not lie in the presence of these desires, but in the behaviors we use to obtain them. Proactive changes are needed to address our physical, emotional, and spiritual needs without hurting others or depriving ourselves of our God-given desires.

Step-Sponsor Prompt

Snapshot

In Exhibit 30 the authors introduce you to the format to be used for Replacement Behaviors Worksheet along with explanations of what is expected in each section. Please review the model as well as the material above before moving on. The Replacement Behaviors Worksheet will provide you with a framework within which you can categorize the behaviors that you will replace with healthy behaviors.

Exhibit: 30
Title: Replacement Behaviors Worksheet
Subtitle: Format

Defect: My problem with …		
Replacement Behaviors	**Now**	**Plan**
Sex/Romance	▨	▨
Money/Material Possessions	▨	▨
Emotional Security	▨	▨
Power/ Status	▨	▨

Replacement Behaviors

The first column titled "Replacement Behaviors" provides examples of commonly reported behavioral changes that have been used to replace the unwanted behaviors of a variety of different defects of character. This is not a list of every possibility and you are encouraged to include your own personal additions in the space provided. The examples have been placed under the heading that the authors believe represents the best fit.

The areas of concentration: Sex/Romance, Money/Material Possessions, Emotional Security, and Power/Status are thought to be the major areas of our life in which our defects of character develop in order to cope with discomfort or unmet needs.

Now

The second and third columns, titled "Now" and "Plan," respectively, provide space for you to check those behaviors that have already been introduced (or that you plan to introduce) into your plan for continued recovery. Place a check in the "Now" column if you have already introduced the behavior into your plan.

Plan

Place a check in the "Plan" column if you intend to introduce the behavior into your plan.

Step-Sponsor Prompt

Snapshot

In Exhibit 31 the authors present the first of two samples for Replacement Behaviors Worksheet that addresses the identification of healthy behaviors to cope with emotional challenges that will replace the behaviors that were eliminated. The first sample deals with an individual problem with coping with the feeling of anger. Please review the two samples before beginning Task 6.

Notes to Myself:

Exhibit: 31
Title: Replacement Behaviors Worksheet
Subtitle: Sample #1

Defect: My problem with coping with anger		
Replacement Behaviors	**Now**	**Plan**
Sex/Romance		
I will keep a daily journal and share what I discover about my moods and feelings with my partner	X	
I will debrief with my partner any event that I found troubling regardless of whether or not she knows about it		X
When I am uncomfortable with my sexuality I will discuss it with my partner		
When I am sexually interested in my partner I will discuss it directly with her		X
Money/Material Possessions		
I will maintain a regular accounting of my finances with my partner	X	
I will develop a budget with the help of all that are influenced by it to eliminate impulse spending		X
I will complete focused Fourth and Fifth Steps on my problem with economic insecurity		X
Emotional Security		
I will use my daily journaling to monitor my emotional and spiritual well-being and report my findings to intimate members of my support system		X
Power/ Status		
I will complete focused Fourth and Fifth Steps on relationships that I find oppressive and develop plans for boundary setting with members of my support system and therapist		X
I will develop an event specific gratitude list with specific attention paid to my accomplishments		X
I will work daily to promote the success of others		X

Step-Sponsor Prompt

Snapshot

In Exhibit 32 the authors present the second sample for Replacement Behaviors Worksheet that addresses the identification of healthy behaviors to cope with emotional challenges that will replace the behaviors that were eliminated. This sample deals with an individual's problem with women. If you are recovering from sex addiction please refer to the Step-Sponsor Prompt Think that appears on page 80 for additional guidance. Please review the two samples before moving on or beginning Task 6.

Exhibit: **32**
Title: **Replacement Behaviors Worksheet**
Subtitle: **Sample # 2**

Defect: My problem with women		
Replacement Behaviors	**Now**	**Plan**
Sex/Romance		
Avoid solitary social contacts with members of the opposite sex when I am in a committed relationship	X	
Let my partner and other members of my support group know who is likely to flirt with me and elicit their help in removing me from harm's way		X
Actively develop a healthy fantasy life which includes a partner in a committed relationship in order to change the structure of my arousal template		X
Tell members of my support group whom I am likely to flirt with and what the behavior will look like so that they can help me interrupt it		X
Upon reaching the 9th Step, prepare and initiate plans to make amends to those I have objectified through flirtation and seductive behavior		X
Enhance number and depth of male support groups		X
Talk to my sponsor and therapist when sexual desires become intrusive		X
Talk to my partner for help when my unwanted sexual desires become intrusive		X
Money/Material Possessions		
Let people I trust know about my history of "deserving" pain and "suffering compensation" and what I look and sound like when I am putting together my "case"		X
Emotional Security		
Make a commitment to let those I trust know when I am uncomfortable		X
Let the people I trust know when I have a fear that they are going to disapprove of something I am thinking, feeling, or have a desire to do		X
Develop a plan of abstinence for each of the substances or behaviors that artificially change my mood and tell those I trust what my plan is	X	
Let those I trust know how to determine that I am isolating and what some of the known triggers are for that behavior		X
Power/ Status		
Look for opportunities in all settings to share my identification with those I encounter as well as my experience, strength, and hope, if it is welcomed	X	
When I am angry, write out what I want to say and read it to God before delivering it to the person I have written it for		
Do not allow others to become overly indebted to me for economic support	X	
When I want to give someone I care for input, ask their permission		X

Step-Sponsor Prompt

Action

Go to Appendix L and complete Replacement Behaviors Worksheet. There are six blank sheets. We limited the number of available sheets in order to encourage you to focus your attention on a limited number of defects. If you need more space attach loose-leaf sheets.

Notes to Myself:

Chapter 2: Preparing a Humble Offering – Step 7

The Seventh Step is a decisive step of surrender much like the Third and Fifth Steps. In the Third Step we surrendered "our will and our lives over to the care of God as we understood him." The text of *Alcoholics Anonymous*[2] (1953, p.59) explains that we were "building a new and triumphant arch through which we passed to freedom." So it was for us when we began to have a spiritual awakening as promised. The stirring of our spirit triggered an equally important emotional awakening, however, as for most people, our suppressed emotions were quite grumpy when they awoke.

The introduction of the Fourth and Fifth Steps created yet another challenge of surrender. We found ourselves facing the need to surrender to God and to another human being the secrets that would keep us as sick as the addictive or co-addictive behaviors had kept us. The completion of a thorough Fourth Step and the accompanying Fifth Step brought a significant degree of relief from the emotional pain of our past and we were grateful to be out of the shadows. The Sixth Step was a natural progression into self-awareness and, although challenging at times, was never unbearable once we actually began in earnest. The Seventh Step completes the fourth part of a five-part *surrender process* that began when we emerged from the Second Step and began to clear away the wreckage of our past.

The Seventh Step is a surrendering of the behaviors we have coveted nearly as much as our drugs of choice themselves. The work you have done thus far has been an effort to demonstrate to the God of your understanding that you are indeed ready to have these defects of character removed. If you have been thorough with your work in the previous six Tasks, you have created a script for changing your future. God will remove those defects of character that you have become willing to remove in their entirety. No more half-measures. No more foxhole prayers in which you promise never to do it again if only you were allowed to escape this current crisis.

We are not making deals with God. We are demonstrating our willingness to start anew without forgetting where we have been. Share all that you have written with a sponsor or spiritual advisor and your romantic partner or a close family member before bringing your offering to the God of your understanding.

The more people who know about your new plan for living, the more help you will receive to avoid the pitfalls of self-will. Ask the members of your support group to hold you accountable for the plan you have prepared in Tasks 5 and 6. The behaviors you identified in Tasks 5 and 6 are not likely to be a surprise to those who know you; but just in case your loved ones do not know about something you plan to eliminate, discuss your disclosure with a sponsor, spiritual advisor, or therapist before you risk hurting someone with your honesty. This rule does not apply to your sponsor, spiritual advisor, or therapist. They should hear your Sixth Step in its entirety.

The Sixth Step you have completed has been an honest beginning, but it will serve you best if you consider it to be a "work in progress." On a yearly basis, or more frequently if needed, you should update each of the 6 Tasks. It will be a great way to measure your emotional and spiritual progress. And you are likely to make important additions to the replacement behaviors as you continue to grow in the knowledge of God's will for you.

Farewell

We hope you have found *Clearing Away the Wreckage of the Past: A Task Oriented Guide for Completing Steps 4 through 7* a worthwhile resource. A decision to surrender those behaviors that stand in the way of your usefulness to you and your fellows will create enormous opportunities for growth. We have tried to provide you with sufficient challenges as well as inspiration and loving support. We hope that you have felt our presence.

We are interested in your comments about the guide and would welcome the opportunity to respond to your inquiries. Contact us at www.leademcounseling.com. If you encounter difficulties with the guide as you are working through the Tasks, you are encouraged to contact us through our web site for brief e-mail support.

The "Seventh Step Prayer" (*Alcoholics Anonymous*[2], 1953, p. 76), as it is commonly referred to in the recovery community, is a fitting way to bid you farewell and Godspeed:

"My Creator, I am now willing that you should have all of me, good and bad. I pray that you now remove from me every single defect of character, which stands in the way of my usefulness to you and my fellows. Grant me strength, as I go out from here, to do your bidding. Amen."

In peace,

John and Elaine Leadem

Leadem Counseling & Consulting Services, P.C.

668 Commons Way

Toms River, New Jersey 08755

732-797-1444

www.leademcounseling.com

Glossary of Terms

Addiction

The phrases addiction or addictive illness are used throughout the guide to refer to the manifestation of an addictive process that may include substances as in the case of alcoholism or behavior patterns such as sex addiction as well as co-addictive disorders. The co-addicted others in the addicted person's life also suffer many of the same symptoms of the illness because of the coping strategies that are developed for living in community with the addicted person. The co-addict's addictive illness can follow the same destructive course as the addicted person.

Bottom

The term *bottom* refers to the subjective point at which the addicted or co-addicted person realizes that he or she can no longer spring back from an addictive episode or is no longer able or willing to accept the consequences of not getting treatment for the addictive illness.

Cork in the Jug

A phrase used in the recovery culture when referring to the inadequacy of merely abstaining from the "drug of choice." If the alcoholic attempts to recover by merely "putting the cork in the jug" he will soon discover that there is a great deal more involved in sustaining sobriety.

Compatible Defects of Character

Defects of character are maladaptive coping strategies that are developed during one's youth to cope with the emotional challenges of life that appear overbearing. Compatible defects of character is a phase that depicts a relationship between two people that is conflicted, in part, because of the tendency for one person's defect of character to appear to trigger the other person's character defect to the foreground. An example of this phenomenon is illustrated in the following sentence. If one person in a relationship chases every opportunity in search of happiness or success he or she is likely to be in a relationship with someone who avoids risk taking at all cost and would prefer to maintain the status quo.

Drug

When *drug* appears it refers to any mood altering addictive substance or behavior that is used or intended to move one from an uncomfortable emotional mood toward euphoria. For some people, the drug is food. For others, it may be the emotional numbing that occurs from controlling others.

Drug of Choice

The idea that drinking alcoholic beverages in general and liquor in specific was only a symptom of the alcoholic's underlying spiritual problem was a critical feature of the 12 Step model. All but the First Step focus the sufferer's attention on the spiritual changes that will be required to ensure sustained freedom from addiction. You only need to replace the word "drinking" with the phrase *return to a state of active addiction*. Your *drug of choice* is a phrase intended to portray the object of an addictive obsession. The alcoholic might think about drinking, the food addict about over or under-eating, the gambler about placing a bet, and victims of other processes addictions will develop desires that fit their own addiction related pattern.

Housecleaning

Housecleaning as it relates to a program of recovery from addiction or co-addiction refers to the process of inventory taking, sharing of secrets, surrendering of maladaptive patterns of behavior, and the making of amends found in Steps 4 through 9.

Program of Recovery

The original 12 Step recovery program text, *Alcoholics Anonymous*[2] uses the term program or the phrase "program of recovery" 19 times and each presentation is referring the reader back to the 12 Steps. Recovery meetings are vital. Anniversary celebrations and the development of a support group are integral aspects of the recovery experience but they are not <u>the program</u>. The program is the 12 Steps.

Promises

There are many rewards promised for those who are painstaking about the practice of the 12 Steps in all their affairs. Some students of recovery have identified over 150 promises in the book *Alcoholics Anonymous*[2] within the first 164 pages alone. The Promises as they are identified in this text refer to the twelve that are highlighted on pages 83 - 84 in *Alcoholics Anonymous*[2] as introduced after the presentation of the Ninth Step. They have been reprinted here for your reference:

> "If we are painstaking about this phase of our development, we will be amazed before we are half way through. We are going to know a new freedom and a new happiness. We will not regret the past nor wish to shut the door on it. We will comprehend the word serenity and we will know peace. No matter how far down the scale we have gone, we will see how our experience can benefit others. That feeling of uselessness and self-pity will disappear. We will lose interest in selfish things and gain interest in our fellows. Self-seeking will slip away. Our whole attitude and outlook upon life will change. Fear of people and of economic insecurity will leave us. We will intuitively know how to handle situations, which used to baffle us. We will suddenly realize that God is doing for us what we could not do for ourselves".

Shared Program of Recovery©[3]

This term, coined by the authors, names a process of integrating the recovery programs and sober practices of partners in a committed relationship. The model represents a sharp departure from the historical notion that family members or loved ones are too close to be of service to each other in pursuit of recovery and that couples, in particular, should stay out of each others' program. The Shared Program of Recovery©[3] model is designed to help partners become intimate members of each other's support system.

Sober Living

The term sober is used throughout this guide with broad reference to mean the life we are building in recovery once abstinence from our addictive substance or behavior has been established.

Surrender Process

The 12 Steps involve a five - part surrender process:

1. In the First Step the addict or co-addict is giving up or surrendering their "drug of choice."

2. The Third Step signals the point at which the addict or co-addict surrenders doing it alone.

3. The Fifth Step brings the addict or co-addict out of the shadows as the secrets are surrendered to another human being.

4. The Seventh Step provides the addict or co-addict with the opportunity to surrender maladaptive coping strategies for healthy ways of coping with their emotions and to develop productive interpersonal relationships.

5. The Twelfth Step encourages the addict or co-addict to apply and practice the previous 11 Steps in all areas of his or her life, surrendering the notion that all will be fine simply because abstinence has been achieved.

Teasing the Addiction

The phrase refers to the practice of engaging in behaviors that, while they do not breach abstinence or violate the addict's or co-addict's "bottom line," would appear to be generating a feeling reward or a vicarious high. Simply speaking, teasing the addiction makes us feel good because it represents a milder form of the "drug of choice" experience. If we are approximating a drug using experience it will not happen without consequence for long. Two examples include: the alcoholic who continues to "party" with her friends and the co-addicted partner who sneaks peaks at his partner's recovery journal. Both are *teasing* their addiction. The eventual cost for *teasing* your addiction could be relapse. *Teasing* your addiction can be a form of harassing your spirit. So remember what you were taught in kindergarten: "don't tease others."

Endnotes

1. All italicized words or phrases (outside of headings) are defined in the glossary of terms that are not cited works.

2. *Alcoholics Anonymous* (3rd ed.). (1953). New York, NY: A.A. World Services, Inc. (A.A.W.S.). The Twelve Steps are reprinted with permission of A.A.W.S., Inc. Permission to reprint the Twelve Steps does not mean that A.A.W.S. necessarily agrees with the views expressed herein. A.A. is a program of recovery from alcoholism only - use of the Twelve Steps in connection with programs and activities which are patterned after A.A., but which address other problems, or in any other non – A.A. context, does not imply otherwise. The references made by page number in this text correspond to pages in 1953 edition of Alcoholics Anonymous with permission of A.A.W.S. The 12 Steps have been reprinted in their entirety for your ease of reference.

3. *Shared Program of Recovery©*. Leadem & Leadem, 2004

Appendix A: Alcoholics Anonymous - The Twelve Steps

1. We admitted we were powerless over alcohol, that our lives had become unmanageable.

2. Came to believe that a Power greater than ourselves could restore us to sanity.

3. Made a decision to turn our will and our lives over to the care of God, as we understood Him.

4. Made a searching and fearless moral inventory of ourselves.

5. Admitted to God, to ourselves, and to another human being the exact nature of our wrongs.

6. Were entirely ready to have God remove all of these defects of character.

7. Humbly asked Him to remove our shortcomings.

8. Made a list of all persons we had harmed, and became willing to make amends to them all.

9. Made direct amends to such people wherever possible, except when to do so would injure them or others.

10. Continued to take personal inventory and when we were wrong, promptly admitted it.

11. Sought through prayer and meditation to improve our conscious contact with God as we understood Him, praying only for knowledge of His will for us and the power to carry that out.

12. Having had a spiritual awakening as the result of these steps, we tried to carry this message to alcoholics, and to practice these principles in all our affairs.

Appendix B: Checklist for Tasks of Component 1

Check off each of the Tasks as you complete them.

- ☐ Create a Master List of every person or institution that has ever wronged you.

- ☐ Create a separate Title Page for each person or institution you have identified on the Master List and place the name of each person or institution on the top of his or her own Title Page.

- ☐ Place the stack of Title Pages in front of you and choose which person or institution to begin with.

- ☐ On the Title Page, for the person or institution that you have chosen, describe, in detail, one of the wrongs that the person or institution has done to you.

- ☐ The guide is designed to use your feeling memories to identify other similar life experiences. Your reflections on the following two questions will remind you of the other people or institutions which have harmed you.

    When have I felt this way?

    Who else has treated me this way?

- ☐ Look at your Master List and identify the people or institutions that have harmed you in a similar fashion. If your reflections on the two questions in Task 5 brought new people or institutions to mind, add them to the Master List and give them their own Title Pages.

- ☐ Pull out the pages for each of the people or institutions that came to mind in Task 5 and identify and describe the wrong that each of them did to you, just as you did in Task 4.

- ☐ When you complete each of the entries for the additional people or institutions, place their pages back in the unfinished pile.

- ☐ Pull the first page back out and continue with the next wrong for that person or institution as you did in Task 4. Each time you add a new wrong for this person or institution, complete Tasks 5, 6, and 7.

- ☐ When you are finished moving back and forth between the various people and institutions, you are finished with Component 1. Do not sit and dig for more material. All the information that God wants you to have for now is out. Call someone and talk if you are stuck. When you are unstuck, continue with Component 2.

Appendix C: Checklist for Tasks of Component 2

Check off each of the Tasks as you complete them.

- ☐ How do these sick people act?
- ☐ In what ways are the personalities of the wrongdoers similar?
- ☐ Are there patterns to the way that I have responded to their sick behavior?
- ☐ What did I hope to get from these people or institutions that they were apparently not ready or able to provide?
- ☐ What is the nature of my relationship with these people today?
- ☐ Do I find myself getting disappointed frequently?
- ☐ Do my relationships appear a bit lopsided?
- ☐ Do I have people in my life today that I allow to get too close to me who are similar to the ones who have hurt me in the past?
- ☐ Who are these sick people and what do I know about their lives?
- ☐ What do I know about the way that the people who harmed me felt or feel about the wrongs that they committed toward me?
- ☐ Can I acquire the humility needed for compassion?
- ☐ Examine how the resentment has injured you.
- ☐ Do my resentments serve a function in my life that I fear I cannot live without?

Appendix D: Checklist for Tasks of Component 3

Check off each of the Tasks as you complete them.

- ☐ Create a Master List of every person or institution that you have ever wronged.

- ☐ Create a separate Title Page for each person or institution you have identified on the Master List and place the name of each person or institution on the top of his or her own Title Page.

- ☐ Place the stack of Title Pages in front of you and choose which person or institution to begin with.

- ☐ On the Title Page, for the person or institution that you have chosen, describe, in detail, one of the wrongs that you have done to that person or institution.

- ☐ The guide is designed to use your feeling memories to identify other similar life experiences. Your reflections on the following two questions will remind you of the other people or institutions which you have harmed.

  When have I felt this way?

  Who else have I treated this way?

- ☐ Look at your Master List and identify the people or institutions you have harmed in a similar fashion. If your reflections on the two questions in Task 5 brought new people or institutions to mind, add them to the Master List and give them their own Title Pages.

- ☐ Pull out the pages for each of the people or institutions that came to mind in Task 5, and identify and describe the wrong that you did to each person or institution just as you did in Task 4.

- ☐ When you complete each of the entries for the additional people or institutions, place their pages back in the unfinished pile.

- ☐ Pull the first page back out and continue with the next wrong for that person or institution as you did in Task 4. Each time you add a new wrong for this person or institution, complete Tasks 5, 6, and 7.

- ☐ When you are finished moving back and forth between the various people and institutions, you are finished with Component 3.

Appendix E: Checklist for Tasks of Component 4

Check off each of the Tasks as you complete them.

- ☐ Which relationships from your combined two Master Lists would you like to improve?

- ☐ What personal character changes will you need to explore in order to make a positive contribution to your relationship with these people?

- ☐ Which relationships do you view as being beyond repair?

- ☐ Which relationships do you need to avoid, if possible, because the relationship is hurtful to you?

Appendix F: Feeling Words

abandoned
absent-minded
abused
accepted
accused
admired
adored
adrift
affectionate
afraid
aggravated
aggressive
agitated
alarmed
alert
alienate
alive
alone
aloof
alluring
amazed
ambushed
amused
angry
antagonistic
anxious
apathetic
appalled
apologetic
appreciated
appreciative
apprehensive
aroused
ashamed
astonished
attacked
attractive
aware
awestruck

awkward
bad
baffled
bashful
beaten down
belittled
benevolent
berated
betrayed
bewildered
bitter
blamed
blue
bold
bored
bothered
brave
broken
bummed
burdened
burned out
calm
capable
carefree
careless
caring
cautious
censored
centered
certain
challenged
charmed
cheated
cheerful
cherished
childish
clean
clear
clever

close
closed
clueless
clumsy
cold
comfortable
committed
compassionate
competent
competitive
complacent
complete
concerned
condemned
confident
confused
considerate
contemplative
contempt
content
controlled
convicted
cornered
courageous
cowardly
cranky
crazy
cross
crushed
curious
daring
dashed
dazed
dead
deceived
dedicated
defeated
defenseless
defensive

defiant	doubtful	flustered
degraded	drained	foolish
dejected	dropped	forgiven
delicate	dull	forgotten
delighted	dumb	fortunate
demoralized	eager	framed
dependent	ecstatic	frantic
depressed	edgy	free
deprived	effective	friendly
deserted	embarrassed	frightened
desired	empathetic	frisky
despair	empty	frustrated
desperate	enchanted	fulfilled
destroyed	encouraged	full
detached	energetic	funny
determined	energized	furious
devastated	elated	generous
devious	enlightened	gentle
devoted	enraged	giving
different	enriched	grieving
difficulty	entertained	glorious
dirty	enthusiastic	good
disappointed	envious	grateful
disbelieving	evasive	great
discarded	evil	glad
disconnected	exasperated	gloomy
discontent	excited	grouchy
discouraged	excluded	grumpy
disgraced	exhausted	guarded
disgusted	exhilarated	guilty
disheartened	expectant	gullible
dishonest	exploited	handicapped
disillusioned	exposed	happy
dismal	exuberant	hateful
dismayed	faithful	haunted
disobedient	fake	healthy
disorganized	fantastic	heard
disposable	fatigued	heartbroken
distant	fearful	helpful
distracted	fearless	helpless
distressed	feisty	hesitant
disturbed	fine	honored

144

hopeful
hopeless
horrible
horrified
hospitable
hostile
humble
humiliated
hurt
hysterical
idealistic
idiotic
ignorant
ignored
imaginative
immune
impatient
impelled
imperfect
impertinent
important
impressed
impulsive
inadequate
inattentive
incensed
incompetent
incomplete
incredulous
indebted
indecisive
independent
industrious
inept
inferior
inflated
informed
infuriated
inhibited
innocent
innovative
inquisitive

insane
insecure
insensitive
insignificant
isolated
insulted
intense
interested
interrogated
interrupted
intimidated
intimate
intrigued
invigorated
invisible
involved
irrational
irresponsible
irritated
irked
jaded
jealous
jinxed
jolly
jovial
joyful
jubilant
judged
judgmental
jumpy
just
justified
kidded
kind
knowledgeable
late
lazy
leery
left out
let down
liable
liberated

lifeless
light-hearted
liked
listened to
logical
lonely
loose
lost
lousy
lovable
loved
loving
lucky
mad
manipulated
mean
meditative
melancholy
merry
mischievous
miserable
misinterpreted
mistreated
misunderstood
mixed up
mocked
molested
moody
motivated
moved
mystified
naïve
nasty
needed
needy
negative
neglected
nervous
neurotic
nonchalant
nostalgic
noticed

numb
obeyed
obligated
obvious
odd
offended
old
open
oppressed
optimistic
ornery
out of control
outraged
overcome
overjoyed
overloaded
overwhelmed
overworked
owned
pampered
paralyzed
passionate
passive
patient
peaceful
peeved
pensive
perky
perplexed
persecuted
pessimistic
pestered
petrified
petty
phony
pious
playful
pleased
poor
possessive
positive
powerful

powerless
practical
pressured
private
productive
protected
protective
proud
provoked
prudish
punished
pushy
puzzled
questioned
quiet
rambunctious
reassured
realistic
rebellious
reborn
receptive
reckless
recognized
reconciled
reflective
refreshed
regretful
rejected
rejuvenated
relaxed
released
relieved
reluctant
reminiscent
remorseful
renewed
replaced
replenished
repressed
rescued
resentful
reserved

resistant
resourceful
respected
responsible
restricted
revengeful
revitalized
rich
ridiculous
right
rigid
robbed
romantic
rotten
rushed
sabotaged
sad
safe
sassy
satisfied
saved
scared
scolded
scorned
secure
seductive
self-assured
self-centered
self-confident
self-conscious
self-destructive
self-reliant
selfish
sensitive
sentimental
serene
serious
sexy
skillful
shamed
shaken
sheepish

shocked	sure	unaccepted
shunned	surly	unappreciated
shy	surprised	unbalanced
sick	suspicious	unburdened
silenced	sympathetic	uncanny
silly	tacky	uncomfortable
sincere	tactful	unconcerned
sinful	talented	uneven
slandered	talkative	unfit
sluggish	tame	unfriendly
small	tarnished	united
smart	tasteful	unjust
smothered	tearful	unknown
skeptical	teased	unneeded
solemn	tenacious	unpleasant
soothed	tender	unreal
sorry	tense	unruly
special	tepid	unwise
spiteful	terrible	uplifted
splendid	terrific	used
spunky	terrified	useless
squashed	thankful	vacant
stifled	thoughtful	vain
stimulated	threatened	vague
stingy	thrifty	valid
strained	thrilled	valued
stretched	tired	vexed
stressed	tormented	vicious
strong	torn	victimized
stubborn	tortured	victorious
stumped	tough	violated
stunned	tragic	vivid
stupid	tranquil	void
submissive	transformed	wacky
successful	trapped	warlike
suicidal	treasured	warm
suffocated	trebly	warmhearted
sullen	tremendous	warned
sunk	tricked	wary
super	troubled	wasted
superior	trusted	weak
supported	ugly	wealthy

weary
weird
whole
wild
willful
wishful
witty
worldly
worse
worthy
wounded
wrong
yearning
yellow
yielding
young
youthful
zany
zealous

Appendix G: Naming the Defect Worksheet

The defect I am targeting is known to me as:

_____

My defect might be known by other names or phrases such as:

_____

_____

_____

If my defect were represented by an animal, it would be:

_____

If my defect had a voice, it would say about me:

_____

_____

_____

_____

If my defect had a voice, it would say about others:

_____

_____

_____

_____

Appendix G: Naming the Defect Worksheet

The defect I am targeting is known to me as:

_____

My defect might be known by other names or phrases such as:

_____

_____

_____

If my defect were represented by an animal, it would be:

_____

If my defect had a voice, it would say about me:

_____

_____

_____

_____

If my defect had a voice, it would say about others:

_____

_____

_____

_____

_____

Appendix G: Naming the Defect Worksheet

The defect I am targeting is known to me as:

_____

My defect might be known by other names or phrases such as:

_____

_____

_____

If my defect were represented by an animal, it would be:

_____

If my defect had a voice, it would say about me:

_____

_____

_____

_____

If my defect had a voice, it would say about others:

_____

_____

_____

_____

Appendix G: Naming the Defect Worksheet

The defect I am targeting is known to me as:

_____

My defect might be known by other names or phrases such as:

_____

_____

_____

If my defect were represented by an animal, it would be:

_____

If my defect had a voice, it would say about me:

_____

_____

_____

_____

If my defect had a voice, it would say about others:

_____

_____

_____

_____

_____

Appendix G: Naming the Defect Worksheet

The defect I am targeting is known to me as:

_____

My defect might be known by other names or phrases such as:

_____

_____

_____

If my defect were represented by an animal, it would be:

_____

If my defect had a voice, it would say about me:

_____

_____

_____

_____

If my defect had a voice, it would say about others:

_____

_____

_____

_____

Appendix G: Naming the Defect Worksheet

The defect I am targeting is known to me as:

_____

My defect might be known by other names or phrases such as:

_____

_____

_____

If my defect were represented by an animal, it would be:

_____

If my defect had a voice, it would say about me:

_____

_____

_____

_____

If my defect had a voice, it would say about others:

_____

_____

_____

_____

Appendix H: Identifying Common Symptoms Worksheet - Page 1

Defect name:

_____

Work/School setting:

_____

_____

_____

_____

In the company of close friends:

_____

_____

_____

_____

In the company of extended family members:

_____

_____

_____

_____

Appendix H: Identifying Common Symptoms Worksheet - Page 2

In the company of my children:

_____

_____

_____

_____

In the company of my spouse:

_____

_____

_____

_____

In the company of my parents:

_____

_____

_____

_____

During sexual or romantic encounters:

_____

_____

_____

_____

Appendix H: Identifying Common Symptoms Worksheet - Page 3

While involved in 12 Step meetings:

_____

_____

_____

_____

When the management of finances is involved:

_____

_____

_____

_____

While involved in 12 Step work:

_____

_____

_____

_____

While dealing with the general public:

_____

_____

_____

_____

Appendix H: Identifying Common Symptoms Worksheet - Page 1

Defect name:

_____

Work/School setting:

_____

_____

_____

_____

In the company of close friends:

_____

_____

_____

_____

In the company of extended family members:

_____

_____

_____

_____

Appendix H: Identifying Common Symptoms Worksheet - Page 2

In the company of my children:

_____

_____

_____

_____

In the company of my spouse:

_____

_____

_____

_____

In the company of my parents:

_____

_____

_____

_____

During sexual or romantic encounters:

_____

_____

_____

_____

Appendix H: Identifying Common Symptoms Worksheet - Page 3

While involved in 12 Step meetings:

_____

_____

_____

_____

When the management of finances is involved:

_____

_____

_____

_____

While involved in 12 Step work:

_____

_____

_____

_____

While dealing with the general public:

_____

_____

_____

_____

Appendix H: Identifying Common Symptoms Worksheet - Page 1

Defect name:

_____

Work/School setting:

_____

_____

_____

_____

In the company of close friends:

_____

_____

_____

_____

In the company of extended family members:

_____

_____

_____

_____

Appendix H: Identifying Common Symptoms Worksheet - Page 2

In the company of my children:

_____

_____

_____

_____

In the company of my spouse:

_____

_____

_____

_____

In the company of my parents:

_____

_____

_____

_____

During sexual or romantic encounters:

_____

_____

_____

_____

Appendix H: Identifying Common Symptoms Worksheet - Page 3

While involved in 12 Step meetings:

_____

_____

_____

_____

When the management of finances is involved:

_____

_____

_____

_____

While involved in 12 Step work:

_____

_____

_____

_____

While dealing with the general public:

_____

_____

_____

_____

Appendix H: Identifying Common Symptoms Worksheet - Page 1

Defect name:

_____

Work/School setting:

_____

_____

_____

_____

In the company of close friends:

_____

_____

_____

_____

In the company of extended family members:

_____

_____

_____

_____

Appendix H: Identifying Common Symptoms Worksheet - Page 2

In the company of my children:

_____

_____

_____

_____

In the company of my spouse:

_____

_____

_____

_____

In the company of my parents:

_____

_____

_____

_____

During sexual or romantic encounters:

_____

_____

_____

_____

Appendix H: Identifying Common Symptoms Worksheet - Page 3

While involved in 12 Step meetings:

_____

_____

_____

_____

When the management of finances is involved:

_____

_____

_____

_____

While involved in 12 Step work:

_____

_____

_____

_____

While dealing with the general public:

_____

_____

_____

_____

Appendix H: Identifying Common Symptoms Worksheet - Page 1

Defect name:

_____

Work/School setting:

_____

_____

_____

_____

In the company of close friends:

_____

_____

_____

_____

In the company of extended family members:

_____

_____

_____

_____

Appendix H: Identifying Common Symptoms Worksheet - Page 2

In the company of my children:

_____

_____

_____

_____

In the company of my spouse:

_____

_____

_____

_____

In the company of my parents:

_____

_____

_____

_____

During sexual or romantic encounters:

_____

_____

_____

_____

Appendix H: Identifying Common Symptoms Worksheet - Page 3

While involved in 12 Step meetings:

_____

_____

_____

_____

When the management of finances is involved:

_____

_____

_____

_____

While involved in 12 Step work:

_____

_____

_____

_____

While dealing with the general public:

_____

_____

_____

_____

Appendix H: Identifying Common Symptoms Worksheet - Page 1

Defect name:

_____

Work/School setting:

_____

_____

_____

_____

In the company of close friends:

_____

_____

_____

_____

In the company of extended family members:

_____

_____

_____

_____

Appendix H: Identifying Common Symptoms Worksheet - Page 2

In the company of my children:

_____

_____

_____

_____

In the company of my spouse:

_____

_____

_____

_____

In the company of my parents:

_____

_____

_____

_____

During sexual or romantic encounters:

_____

_____

_____

_____

Appendix H: Identifying Common Symptoms Worksheet - Page 3

While involved in 12 Step meetings:

_____

_____

_____

_____

When the management of finances is involved:

_____

_____

_____

_____

While involved in 12 Step work:

_____

_____

_____

_____

While dealing with the general public:

_____

_____

_____

_____

Appendix I: Reviewing the Bill Worksheet

Defect: My problem with …

Area & Items	Past	Now	Long-Term Impact/Future Cost
Sex/Romance			
Money/Material Possessions			
Emotional Security			
Power/ Status			

Appendix I: Reviewing the Bill Worksheet

Defect: My problem with …			
Area & Items	**Past**	**Now**	**Long-Term Impact/Future Cost**
Sex/Romance			
Money/Material Possessions			
Emotional Security			
Power/ Status			

Appendix I: Reviewing the Bill Worksheet

Defect: My problem with …			
Area & Items	**Past**	**Now**	**Long-Term Impact/Future Cost**
Sex/Romance			
Money/Material Possessions			
Emotional Security			
Power/ Status			

Appendix I: Reviewing the Bill Worksheet

Defect: My problem with …			
Area & Items	**Past**	**Now**	**Long-Term Impact/Future Cost**
Sex/Romance			
Money/Material Possessions			
Emotional Security			
Power/ Status			

Appendix I: Reviewing the Bill Worksheet

Defect: My problem with ...			
Area & Items	**Past**	**Now**	**Long-Term Impact/Future Cost**
Sex/Romance			
Money/Material Possessions			
Emotional Security			
Power/ Status			

Appendix I: Reviewing the Bill Worksheet

Defect: My problem with …			
Area & Items	**Past**	**Now**	**Long-Term Impact/Future Cost**
Sex/Romance			
Money/Material Possessions			
Emotional Security			
Power/ Status			

Appendix J: Assessing the Payoff Worksheet

Defect: My problem with …		
Benefit/Payoff	**Past**	**Now**
Sex/Romance	////	////
Money/Material Possessions	////	////
Emotional Security	////	////
Power/ Status	////	////

Appendix J: Assessing the Payoff Worksheet

Defect: My problem with …		
Benefit/Payoff	**Past**	**Now**
Sex/Romance		
Money/Material Possessions		
Emotional Security		
Power/ Status		

Appendix J: Assessing the Payoff Worksheet

Defect: My problem with ...		
Benefit/Payoff	**Past**	**Now**
Sex/Romance	▨	▨
Money/Material Possessions	▨	▨
Emotional Security	▨	▨
Power/ Status	▨	▨

Appendix J: Assessing the Payoff Worksheet

Defect: My problem with …		
Benefit/Payoff	**Past**	**Now**
Sex/Romance	////	////
Money/Material Possessions	////	////
Emotional Security	////	////
Power/ Status	////	////

Appendix J: Assessing the Payoff Worksheet

Defect: My problem with …		
Benefit/Payoff	**Past**	**Now**
Sex/Romance	////////	////////
Money/Material Possessions	////////	////////
Emotional Security	////////	////////
Power/ Status	////////	////////

Appendix J: Assessing the Payoff Worksheet

Defect: My problem with …		
Benefit/Payoff	**Past**	**Now**
Sex/Romance	/////	/////
Money/Material Possessions	/////	/////
Emotional Security	/////	/////
Power/ Status	/////	/////

Appendix K: The Things We Must Change Worksheet

Defect: My problem with …		
Behaviors to Eliminate/Change	**Past**	**Now**
Sex/Romance	▨	▨
Money/Material Possessions	▨	▨
Emotional Security	▨	▨
Power/ Status	▨	▨

Appendix K: The Things We Must Change Worksheet

Defect: My problem with ...		
Behaviors to Eliminate/Change	**Past**	**Now**
Sex/Romance	▨	▨
Money/Material Possessions	▨	▨
Emotional Security	▨	▨
Power/ Status	▨	▨

Appendix K: The Things We Must Change Worksheet

Defect: My problem with …		
Behaviors to Eliminate/Change	**Past**	**Now**
Sex/Romance	▨	▨
Money/Material Possessions	▨	▨
Emotional Security	▨	▨
Power/ Status	▨	▨

Appendix K: The Things We Must Change Worksheet

Defect: My problem with …		
Behaviors to Eliminate/Change	**Past**	**Now**
Sex/Romance	▨	▨
Money/Material Possessions	▨	▨
Emotional Security	▨	▨
Power/ Status	▨	▨

Appendix K: The Things We Must Change Worksheet

Defect: My problem with …		
Behaviors to Eliminate/Change	**Past**	**Now**
Sex/Romance	////	////
Money/Material Possessions	////	////
Emotional Security	////	////
Power/ Status	////	////

Appendix K: The Things We Must Change Worksheet

Defect: My problem with …		
Behaviors to Eliminate/Change	**Past**	**Now**
Sex/Romance		
Money/Material Possessions		
Emotional Security		
Power/ Status		

Appendix L: Replacement Behaviors Worksheet

Defect: My problem with …		
Replacement Behaviors	**Past**	**Now**
Sex/Romance		
Money/Material Possessions		
Emotional Security		
Power/ Status		

Appendix L: Replacement Behaviors Worksheet

Defect: My problem with …		
Replacement Behaviors	**Past**	**Now**
Sex/Romance	////	////
Money/Material Possessions	////	////
Emotional Security	////	////
Power/ Status	////	////

Appendix L: Replacement Behaviors Worksheet

Defect: My problem with …		
Replacement Behaviors	**Past**	**Now**
Sex/Romance	////	////
Money/Material Possessions	////	////
Emotional Security	////	////
Power/ Status	////	////

Appendix L: Replacement Behaviors Worksheet

Defect: My problem with …		
Replacement Behaviors	**Past**	**Now**
Sex/Romance		
Money/Material Possessions		
Emotional Security		
Power/ Status		

Appendix L: Replacement Behaviors Worksheet

Defect: My problem with …		
Replacement Behaviors	**Past**	**Now**
Sex/Romance	////////	////////
Money/Material Possessions	////////	////////
Emotional Security	////////	////////
Power/ Status	////////	////////

Appendix L: Replacement Behaviors Worksheet

Defect: My problem with …		
Replacement Behaviors	**Past**	**Now**
Sex/Romance	▨	▨
Money/Material Possessions	▨	▨
Emotional Security	▨	▨
Power/ Status	▨	▨

About the Authors

Elaine and John Leadem are natives of New Jersey who have recently returned to the beach community they longed to call home since their childhood. The decision to answer the call of the Atlantic Laughing Gulls evolved from a commitment to aid their beloved Aunt Kay who shared their yearning to be near the calming sounds of the surf. Aunt Kay passed away before the relocation could be completed and this work and those that will follow are dedicated to her out of gratitude for all that she gave to others.

The Leadem's are Licensed Clinical Social Workers whose combined investment in the field of addiction treatment spans over 60 years. A service based passion for their work has taken them into every modality conceivable for treating addictive and co-addictive disorders. They maintain a commitment to personal and professional growth that is grounded in state of the art treatment methodology and a core belief in the spiritual principles embedded in the 12 Step philosophy of recovery from addictive disorders. They are committed to leading by example and proudly acknowledge that they would never ask of a client more than they have accomplished themselves.

In addition to being the co-directors of Leadem Counseling & Consulting Services, a rapidly expanding private clinical practice providing therapeutic services from marriage and family therapy to intervention training, Elaine and John are seasoned therapeutic retreat masters. Their work with recovering couples has created a unique blue print for recovery that their clients nicknamed a *Shared Program of Recovery©*. The name and the model produced the framework for the first in a series of meditation guides published under the title: *One In the Spirit: A Meditation Course for Recovering Couples.*

This guide for completing Steps 4 through 7 is intended to be a companion task-by-task workbook to a series of inspirational guides the authors are preparing for publication by Gentle Path Press. Their first contribution to the series, *Surveying the Wreckage* is available at www.leademcounseling.com. This and other works, available for purchase, was inspired by the authors' sustained commitment to practice the principles of recovery *in all their affairs*. Their combined tenure in recovery that totals over 75 years will be celebrated by their commitment to remain newcomers.

About the Artist

The cover art was provided by Julia M. Ratushny, who has an amazing gift for capturing the beauty of the New Jersey coastline in watercolor. If you are interested in seeing more of her work please visit her website at www.julieratushny.com.

Made in the USA
Columbia, SC
17 January 2019